A SLICE OF SUFFOLK

BY THE SAME AUTHOR

Breeze for a Bargeman.   Terence Dalton Limited
Rough and Tumble.   Mallard Reprints
Coasting Bargemaster.   Mallard Reprints
Last of the Sailormen.   Routledge and Kegan Paul

A SLICE OF SUFFOLK

by

BOB ROBERTS

Foreword by John Seymour

TERENCE DALTON LIMITED

LAVENHAM . SUFFOLK

1978

Published by

TERENCE DALTON LIMITED

ISBN 0 86138 020 7

First published 1978
Second Impression 1982
Third Impression 1990

Text photoset in 11/12 pt. Baskerville

Printed in Great Britain at
The Lavenham Press Limited, Lavenham, Suffolk

Contents

Index of Illustrations

*　*　*　*　*　*　*　*　*　*

All drawings by Anne Roberts

*　*　*　*　*　*　*　*　*　*

To the people of Suffolk

Author's Preface

THIS little book is intended to give the reader a taste of Suffolk. I have avoided the "guide-book" style involving tedious dates and figures and although I have culled a little material from official history, these ancient stories do not come from the University fact-collector. They are from family letters and documents, cottage-hidden treasures, conversations with all and sundry, and fascinating word-of-mouth folklore which is often at odds with the history book.

I have collected and written the material, which now forms this book, over a period of twenty-five years. Many of my informants and helpers have passed away and it is impossible now to name them all personally. Many of them would not wish to be named, but I am grateful to them nevertheless. Visits to many museums and libraries have sometimes revealed tit-bits which link old legends to facts.

Particularly am I indebted to the help and patience of the Admiralty librarians in descriptions of the attacks on England by the Dutch Admiral de Ruyter.

The scholar may dispute my interpretation of past events but this may sharpen the appetite of the reader to see and hear more of this ancient land and people. Suffolk is different, its natives are different, its language is different—not a bit like "the Shires", as they call the rest of England.

Pray do not read this as a history, but savour it as **A Slice of Suffolk** through Suffolk eyes, where past and present are one, and never divided into modern times and historical facts.

Bob Roberts,
Ryde,
Isle of Wight
July, 1978.

Foreword

CAPTAIN A. W. Roberts, known to high and low as Bob, has a sense of history like nobody else I know. History to him is not something divorced from the real world in which we live. We are part of it — it is part of us. When he pokes the nose of his ship into some Continental port, he does so remembering that he is only the last one of a long line of traders who have carried English goods in there, or troops perhaps of an invading army. When he sails back across the narrow seas he remembers the Gauls, the Romans, the English, the Vikings and the Normans who all made the same sort of voyages, wave after wave of settlers, raiders, traders, invaders and conquerors to these islands. I have stood with him many times on the deck of *Cambria*, the sailing barge that he was Master of for so many years, sailing into some East Coast estuary, and I know he never did so without remembering other sailors of other days, feeling their way carefully into uncharted waters with the lead line and their inborn experience.

It might be said that an historian should be unpartisan. This could never be said of Bob Roberts — he is the least unpartisan man I know. He thinks, feels, lives and writes as an Englishman. This gives him, as it happens, great strength in studying history — he really *feels* it — any happening of the past that concerns his own race is vivid to him. He views the Battle of Hastings as a personal affront. If *only* Harold had been less impatient — had stopped after his forced march from the North to rally his forces — had lured the Normans further inland and then fallen on them and slain them! I have a secret belief that he would rather like us to fight that battle over again and this time win it!

And indeed his very partisanship for the English makes him able to understand other nations better. He stands on a firm fixed base when he considers other countries and their inhabitants. He is fair to other countries. Provided they respect his Englishness he will respect their Dutchness, Danishness, Frenchness, Welshness or whatever else it is. He writes history as a participant — not as a disembodied observer of phenomena that don't really concern him.

And in his writing about the parts of East Anglia that he intimately knows, in this book, he makes use of this living sense of history in a marvellous manner. As he points out, many of the very old people he used to talk to, thirty years ago perhaps, had memories which stretch back from our time now nearly a hundred years, and they would talk to him about the memories of their parents — and even grandparents — which stretched back to the Battle of Waterloo. During the last fifty years — since the writer of this book has been an adult — the human world has changed faster than in all the rest of its history put together. Captain Roberts shines the light of living memory right back before this time, when rural life appeared to be unchanging, when men and women lived in organic relation with the soil, when sailors really sailed, making use of winds and tides and instinct and intelligence to take them and their vessels to where they wanted to go.

However pleased we are with the present we cannot, except at our peril, ignore our past. And this book brings the past up bright and living before us, as no painstaking list of facts and items dragged out of the County Archives can ever do.

This is living history — a history of which we are still part and which is still going on and I cannot imagine any Anglo-Saxon — any European for that matter — who would not achieve a keener sense of what he is and where he came from by reading this book.

JOHN SEYMOUR
Fachongle Isaf
Wales

CHAPTER ONE

On Ancient Times

A THOUSAND years ago, in Anglo-Saxon times, the shallow River Pindle rattled and chattered its way over the stones and pebbles which for centuries had been washed down between the wooded slopes of Suffolk, gushing cheerfully into the River Orwell some five miles south-east of Gippeswyke—the Ipswich of later years. Too shallow for a boat at most times, but deep enough to launch one at its mouth at high water.

On the west bank of the Pindle stood a mill, one of three on that side of the Orwell, the others being at Shotley, near the sea, and Stoke, close by Gippeswyke on a grassy rise on the left of what is now called Vernon Road.

Around the mouth of the Pindle, in addition to the mill were scattered thatched hovels and cottages where a few fishermen, boat-builders and hunters lived. There was also at least one potter, for the clay in the local soil suited his purpose. The old Angles who inhabited these parts were fair craftsmen in the art by the standards of those times; expert enough to excite the envy of the Norsemen. When the dragon ships came plunging into the eastern rivers their crews eventually settled among their English cousins and the East Anglian potters taught them their trade.

Perhaps the Iceni and Trinovantes, ancient British tribes whose origins were in the Rhineland and Gaul, taught the English, the English taught the Danes, and the Anglo-Danes taught the comparatively barbaric Normans. This seems to be the simple story of East Anglian pottery and almost every excavation in the Ipswich area in recent years reveals samples of their wares.

On the east side of the Pindle was a small wooden quay and landing place—and possibly an ale house of sorts because on the site of the present *Butt and Oyster Inn* there seems to have been a place of liquid refreshment since the beginning of time, and quite certainly for some six hundred years. In 1340 Prince Edward's soldiery, massing with a fleet of three hundred ships in the Orwell before sailing for Flanders to win the great naval Battle of Sluys, were lodged and refreshed at ale houses on the banks of the river and no doubt the ancestor of the *Butt and Oyster* had its share of a roaring and uproarious trade.

In 1968, when the sewer pipes were being laid, workmen digging down in the roadway opposite the top of the Hard came across heavy oak beams, black and hard as rock, some six feet below the surface. But the tides were filling their trench and with the pumps going full bore, there was little opportunity for the historically minded to investigate. But the beams certainly looked like a cross-section of an old quay opposite the eastern corner of the *Butt* garage.

Before the Norman Conquest, Ipswich was divided between Edward the Confessor's Queen Eadgyth, sister of Harold, the tragic hero of Hastings, and her brother Gyrth, who was Earl of East Anglia. The Earldom of East Anglia was at that time almost equivalent to the present office of Prince of Wales, and

The *Butt and Oyster* from the Hard. Pin Mill.

its holder was in direct line for the Crown of England. Gyrth, whose father Earl Godwin had been a favourite at the Court of King Canute and had long connections with Essex and Suffolk, was, it seems, a better military strategist than his impetuous brother Harold.

Had Gyrth's advice been taken there might never have been a Norman Conquest. The English had won a bloody battle at Stamford Bridge in the north and Gyrth urged Harold to wait in London for fresh troops rather than rush headlong into battle against the redoubtable Knights of Normandy. And even on the tragic hill of Sandelake, or Senlac as the Normans called it, he all but brought about the downfall of the mighty Duke. As William rode up shouting challenges to Harold to step out and fight, Gyrth, who bore a striking resemblance to his royal brother, came forward and aimed a mighty stroke with his battle-axe which missed the Duke but felled his charger. Alas, Gyrth slipped on the bloody turf and was left wide open to a mortal blow from William's sword. But for that slip our local Earl, who had so often hunted in the woods and fields of the Shotley Peninsula, fished in the Orwell, and feasted in his house at Ipswich, might have changed the whole course of British history. Perhaps for the better? Who knows?

Woe betide the folk of the Ipswich district when William's Normans drove into the town. The whole place was burnt, cattle slaughtered, and wells poisoned in revenge on the dead Gyrth and the Godwin family. Townsfolk fled to the woods and many, no doubt, lived like hunted animals in the woods and thickets beside the River Pindle.

> Cruel and bloody hand
> Rule the English land

wrote Thorkell Skallason, a contemporary bard.

In those ancient times East Anglia was thickly populated and continued to be for several centuries, although the countryside along the banks of the Orwell was mapped as nothing more exciting than "woods and pasture". This "woods and pasture" character continued uninterrupted even after the coming of the Flemish weavers and the setting up of wealthy town churches and halls. "Woods and pasture" was all the hinterland of Pin Mill could boast of.

Apart from the gathering of the great English Fleet in the Orwell under Edward the Third, the only local event worth noting was the building of Freston Tower in the reign of Henry the Eighth. There was a small manor in those days by Freston hills, and in it lived stern old Hugh de Freston; a Fleming some say, and he was perhaps one of the early links which were to develop between Holland and East Anglia. The "Dutch" Frisians had a foothold in East Anglia even in Saxon times, and villages with names like Freston, Friston and Fressingfield indicate their settlements. A branch of the Anglo-Saxon-Danish tribes, the Frisians were the principal operators of such merchant ships as then plied the North Sea trade. Quite likely Hugh de Freston originally had the tower built as a lookout for his home-coming ships. But as it may have been altered or even rebuilt there is reasonable evidence to suggest that it was re-designed by a young Ipswich builder, Will Latimer, for the education of the beautiful Ellen de Freston, Hugh's golden-haired daughter. We have a record of the use to which the seven chambers, one above the other, were put, the fair Ellen's daily timetable of study being as follows: —

1. 7 a.m. to 8 a.m. . . . . Charity
2. 8 a.m. to 10 a.m. . . . . Tapestry
3. 10 a.m. to noon . . . . Music
4. noon to 1 p.m. . . . . Painting
5. 1 p.m. to 2 p.m. . . . . Literature
6. Evening . . . . Astronomy

One local folk tale is that Will Latimer, having completed the tower, fell in love with Ellen, and the couple were discovered in each others arms on the top floor — and they weren't studying astronomy, either. *She* might have been, but *he* wasn't!

A short distance down river from Freston Tower is a buoy marked "Downham", indicating Downham reach. It is a very narrow part of the river, with barely room for a barge to make a board, and this is what used to be called Downham "Bridge". It was not a bridge in the ordinary sense of the word, but a hard crossing for horses and wagons at low water. The Orwell was shallower in the old days and its bottom shaped more like a saucer, than the ditch-like dredged channel of modern times. And at Downham a crossing could be made. Possibly it was an ancient British highway leading from the territory of the Iceni, which stretched southwards as far as the village of Iken on the banks of the River Alde, to the land of the Trinovantes, who were constantly at war with them. In fact Boadicea's ancestors co-operated with the Romans in the subjugation of the Trinovantes. It was only when the Romans, in a later era, forgot the help the Iceni had given them and became insultingly arrogant that the tall fair-haired tribesmen, who were possibly of Germanic and Celtic stock, turned on them and stormed through the eastern counties like hell let loose. Whether the present day East Anglian has any Iceni blood in his veins is a matter for argument, but it certainly doesn't do to upset him. If you do, "up comes Suffolk" as the local saying is — a thing incoming strangers can neither understand nor overcome.

Downham Bridge was undoubtedly the shallowest part of the Orwell for centuries, and ships bound to Ipswich had to wait for three hours flood tide to lift them over it so that they could proceed up to the town quays. At the time of the Great Plague, ships from London were not allowed up above Downham for fear of infecting the town.

Freston Tower.

A man always on the lookout for incoming ships was an Ipswich wine importer known as Robert le Chaucer. He was a wealthy man and sent his son to be brought up in the household of the Duke of Richmond in Yorkshire. This son was later to become the famed English poet Geoffrey Chaucer, the first man of the literary world to discard the Norman tongue and write in the language of his East Anglian forefathers.

An interesting line in Geoffrey Chaucer's *Canterbury Tales* is his reference to the Shipman, who knew

> every creek in Brittainy and Spain
> His barge was called the Maudelayne.

A Suffolk historian, W. J. Arnott, in 1954 went to great pains to make a list of all the ships based or built on the Orwell from 1295, when a galley was built at Ipswich for Edward the First. Mr Arnott discovered that in 1356 there

Pin Mill Hard.

was an Ipswich victualling ship named the *Maudeleyne*. Was this the vessel young Geoffrey had in mind when he wrote the Shipman's tale? Was she his father's ship carrying chausses of wine from Spain? The name Chaucer came from the fact that his father's wine was brought in chausses which were much the same as the wooden casks of today.

The Civil War had no disastrous impact on a prosperous Suffolk — "selig Suffolk" to use the old term, not "silly Suffolk" as the ignoramuses would have it. In fact so little happened that we must tumble down through the years so rapidly that we come almost to times within living memory of those not long deceased. The late Bernard Cordon of the *East Anglian Daily Times* could remember interviewing an old lady at Woolverstone on her hundredth birthday, and she could remember her grandmother coming into the kitchen and saying, "The Scots have got to Derby, but the Duke of Cumberland is on his way north to drive them out".

The *Butt and Oyster*, Pin Mill

7

CHAPTER TWO

Old Legends, Songs and a Ghost or Two

SOMETIMES in Suffolk time seems to stand still. Old inhabitants have been known to refer quite naturally and without any sense of the extraordinary to events in stories which are centuries old.

There are folk tales and legends in and around Pin Mill which are not dug up from ancient archives, but perpetuated by word of mouth from generation to generation over the centuries, right into the living present. One concerns the church tower at Chelmondiston. When it was first built in the fifteenth(?) century it was said to have been cursed by a witch because she thought that the raising of the tower would reduce her own powers over good and evil. And being thus cursed the tower duly caught fire and was destroyed.

Next a more substantial tower was erected but years later this was struck by lightning and crumbled to the ground. Once more the local masons set to work and put up a fine solid stone tower, so well constructed and on such good foundations as to defy any curse the old witch might have put on it. And there it stood for hundreds of years — the witch and the curse forgotten by all but a few.

Then came the Second World War. And in 1944 a flying bomb came hurtling across the North Sea, struck the tower and exploded. The tower was down again — the rest of the church and the little school next door destroyed as well, by the blast.

The war over, the entire church was rebuilt on the same lines as the old one and its square tower rears up like a sentinel on the hilltop.

How long will it stand this time?

Across the river, at Nacton, there was once fought a fierce battle between East Anglians under their famous Earl Ulfcytel and the invading Danes. The Anglians were well outnumbered but it was one of the hardest local engagements ever fought; and although in the end the Danes "held the field", they suffered such grievous losses that they could take no more effective military action for over a year, until reinforcements arrived from overseas. Danish sagas record that they had never met such "hard sword-play" as they did on that occasion. The bold Earl Ulfcytel was later killed in another desperate battle fought against Canute at Ashingdon in Essex.

On the site of this terrible fight, there are now what are called the Seven Hills. Miss Gill Pretyman, from Orwell Place, took me along to see them. "There are actually eight hills," she said, "I got some help once and had a dig into the hills but found nothing."

These hills are only little mounds. Are they burial places of those slain in the battle? Or do they hold even greater secrets akin to the ship burial at Sutton Hoo? But if you have a sensitive ear and a good imagination, stand quietly by one of the Seven (eight) Hills on the night of an August moon. The nearest one is just off the eastern side of the Ipswich-Felixstowe main road.

The only other strange tale is of a galloping horse at Freston Cross Roads. The late Miss Annie Powell, when she was eighty, told me: "My brother heard it. He came home late from Ipswich. Properly shook him. There was these hooves thundering along right close to him and nothing to be seen — nothing."

Chelmondiston Church of St Andrew, rebuilt on the same lines as the old one, which was destroyed by a German flying bomb.

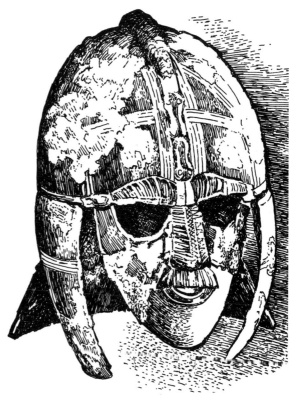

East Anglian King's helmet from the Sutton Hoo Treasure.

Ship burial at Sutton Hoo, Suffolk. Seventh-century A.D. gold buckle with niello inlay

Old Bob Ruffles, the barge skipper, who lived to be well over ninety and whose family were the last malsters at Pin Mill, said: "I walked home that way many a time and I reckoned all this talk about a galloping horse was a lot of old rubbish—till I heard it myself. But I couldn't see no horse."

Some of the life and history of this part of Suffolk is reflected in the old songs which, occasionally, can still be heard, mostly in out-of-the-way inns of a winter evening. The odd stranger is made welcome; but not noisy holiday makers, tape recorders and people who haven't the courtesy to keep silent at the call of "The singer's on his feet". In one old pub where traditional dances and ancient songs were the order of every Saturday night, the intrusion of strangers resulted in a stony silence and a quiet "crib night".

Pin Mill, when it was inhabited mostly by bargemen and fishermen, and yachtsmen were a rarity, used to have one old favourite called the "Princess Royal". This was a song about a ship which once served as a packet boat between Harwich and Flushing. She is shown in an old panoramic print of Harwich Harbour, or Orwell Haven as it was called then. When her packet boat days were ended, this fast little vessel went away on a voyage to Newfoundland and the song tells of how a pirate tried to stop her but found that he could not catch up with her.

> "They chased us to windward
> All night and all day
> They chased us to leeward
> But made no headway
> They fired shots after us
> But none could prevail
> And the bold Princess Royal
> Soon showed 'em her tail."

Pirate ships and packet boats were in a different class when it came to fast sailing. Folk song enthusiasts have recorded and written down a song called the "Princess Royal", but it is not the same as the old Pin Mill version, which was sung to a tune almost, but not quite, the same as another local favourite — "The Yellow Handkerchief".

> "Take this yellow handkerchief
> In rememberance of me."

My grand-uncle, Captain Louis Brown, who was born at Kessingland but often stayed with relations at Pin Mill, used to sing a song about a local ploughboy named Jonas, who sold his soul to the Devil for a hundred pounds. It's a dismal chant rather than a song and how far back the origins of it are no one seemed to know. It is far too long to quote here in full but the latter part of the first verse sets the scene.

> "Weary of the autumn ploughing
> Weary of his arduous call
> Jonas felt a nudge beside him
> Twas the Devil, horns and all.
>
> Sell to me your soul my Jonas
> For a hundred golden pounds
> No more ploughing, no more toil
> Drink your wine and ride to hounds."

11

Captain Louis Brown, world wide navigator, Arctic explorer, adventurer, fisherman. Born at Kessingland, died at Beccles, grand-uncle of the author. On one of his voyages he was away for seven years.

So Jonas sold his soul to the Devil, only to regret it when the hundred pounds was all nearly spent on a pure white palfrey and wines, "rich and rare".

> "Dark and drear remorse struck Jonas
> Wished he had not left his kine
> Master Devil always calling
> Soon now Jonas, you'll be mine."

So Jonas does a deal with the Devil, giving him back what little remained on condition that he sailed away to sea "never to come home again". But the Devil tricked poor Jonas and when the ship came to take the ploughboy away she was manned by a hellish crew with tails and cloven feet.

> "Sadly to the strand went Jonas
> With the Devil at his side
> There's the lofty ship you'll sail in
> Dropping on the falling tide.
>
> Then the longboat came for Jonas
> Took him from his native shore
> Once aboard the bark, poor Jonas
> Stared in terror and in awe.
>
> All the crew were horned and ghastly
> Hauling on the topsail sheet
> And from out their breeks he noticed
> There were tails and cloven feet."

So the hell-ship takes poor Jonas down through the depths to the fiery Hades. A lesson to all simple ploughboys not to trust the Devil.

There is also a local version of an ancient song called "The Smuggler's Boy". It belongs to Stuart times, when liquor was heavily taxed but could be had duty free in Holland and run across to the Suffolk coast at night.

> "My father and mother so happy did dwell
> In a trim little cottage by the River Orwell,
> But my father would venture out on the salt sea
> For a keg of good brandy from the land of the free."*
>
> From Holland we steered but the tempest did roar
> And the lightning flashed round us when far from the shore
> The mast and the rigging were thrown to the wave
> And with them went father to a watery grave."

The lad was washed ashore and saved, but his mother died of grief. And if you can have a happy ending to such a sad song, it is that he was taken in and cared for by "a lady of fortune" who had no children of her own. The last line says,

> "So this poor smuggler boy in my bosom shall bide."

* * *

*Meaning duty-free Holland.

Smuggling was once part of everyday life in the villages bordering the Orwell and the Stour. Everyone was involved to some degree—even parsons who were partial to a decent drop of brandy or Flemish wine, and turned a blind eye to the use of their churches as temporary hiding places for illicit tubs. Shotley was notorious and the use of the church by the "free traders" as they were called, gave rise to the local jingle:—

> Shotley Church
> Without a steeple
> Drunken parson
> Wicked people

Most of the smuggling was well organised and the gangs ashore had recognised centres at Hadleigh, Ipswich, Thetford and Bury St Edmunds, from which places transport ponies and armed escorts could be obtained. At one time scores of ponies were kept grazing on Rushmere Heath (just outside Ipswich) and if the Excisemen observed that a lot were missing they knew that somewhere in the locality a big "run" was being made. But when it came to getting information, the country folk were tight-lipped and blind-eyed. They had seen nothing.

> Face the wall, my darling
> While the gentlemen go by.

This was what the peasant told his daughter so that she could honestly reply to the Excise Officers that she had not seen any "pony train" pass that way.

Pin Mill, of course, with its sheltered beaches and woodlands, was always deeply involved and at Woolverstone there was once a bloody skirmish on the foreshore resulting in the deaths of three local lads who might well have been the occupants of the three nameless graves unearthed when Woolverstone Church was restored.

Officially, a smuggler who met his death resisting the law was treated as a pirate and could not be buried in consecrated ground. Generally his last resting place was a rough grave on the foreshore. But the deep religious fervour of those days often resulted in the mothers pleading with the parson to allow their wayward sons to be buried in the churchyard and this the worthy gentleman often allowed on condition that no names should mark the grave. So on the Day of Judgement the slain smugglers would emerge with all the other Christians and stand some chance of escaping damnation.

Margaret Catchpole became a name known far beyond the banks of the River Orwell after the Reverend Mr Cobbold wrote a story woven round her association with the notorious Will Laud, from Aldeburgh, who sailed for a "free-trade" merchant at Pin Mill. A Nacton girl, Margaret worked at Priory

Farm (opposite Freston) and was eventually convicted of horse stealing after an attempt to join Will Laud in London. The death sentence was commuted to deportation to Australia, where she died. There is a photograph of her grave in Christchurch Museum, Ipswich. But it seems that her life was not quite so romantic as Mr Cobbold would have us believe. Letters from Australia to her former mistress are little more than self-pitying pleas for money. Will Laud, with a price on his head, was shot dead on the beach at Orfordness while trying to escape abroad with Margaret.

But at Pin Mill smuggling was carried on though in different circumstances right up to recent times. Dutchmen used to transfer quantities of gin to local fishing boats and barges off the West Rocks and this was brought right into the village by devious means. The late Mrs Higgins (a barge skipper's daughter), told me that she remembers the Customs and Excise men coming down to Pin Mill one day in 1910 convinced that a good deal of gin had been brought ashore. The bargemen and fishermen were engaged in dredging up coprolite, which the local people called Roman stone, when they had taken the illicit gin. The smack-type boats were called stone-dredgers, and they always left some on the mud at Shotley Spit to make a hard for walking ashore. It is

A smuggler's grave in the churchyard of Woolverstone.

still called "The Stoneheaps". Now it was the usual practice for these men to take their food and necessities to sea with them in a large canvas kit-bag. These they used to hang on the rail of the *Old Butt* quay, as they were too cumbersome to take into the bar. It was a common sight, Mrs Higgins said, to see as many as thirty or more bags hitched on to the quay rail.

When the Customs men were sighted coming down from Chelmondiston, the alarm was raised in the *Butt* and the jars of gin hurriedly stuffed into the kit-bags on the quay. The kit-bags were empty because the womenfolk used to bring the food down and put it in their menfolk's bags when they knew the weather was suitable for them to sail away.

Back in the *Butt* they all resumed drinking as the Customs walked in to search for the gin. Finding nothing there, they went off and searched every barge and boat lying off at anchor. The row of fat kit-bags on the quay rail did not interest them as they were always there and would only be full of food. So the law departed and as soon as the all clear was given the wives came down with the food and departed heavily laden with jars of gin.

The late Captain Harry Rands, a local barge skipper, who died in 1969 at the age of eighty-two, told me that he remembered a cottage being pulled down near Harkstead, and under the kitchen the demolition men found a rough timber cellar stacked with old demijohns of gin.

"I tasted some," he said, "and it was good stuff. I reckoned it was a tidy age and worth a lot of money."

The outgoing tenants had lived there for fifty years and never knew about the treasure under the kitchen floor!

A local seafaring family named Lucas was often in trouble with the Excisemen and it is recorded that one of them, caught red-handed, had to suffer the punishment of having his boat sawn in half on Pin Mill Hard. It was possible, of course to persuade those employed to do the sawing (no doubt with the aid of some excellent liquor) to so perform their task that the boat could easily be put together again, making the saw-cuts at the butts of the planking.

With so much boat building going on in places like Pin Mill it was inevitable that some of the craft were designed for the smuggling trade. In such a case the vessel was termed as being "built for a stranger", instead of the usual "for the Navy" or for "such and such a merchant" or for "the coaling trade".

On one occasion in 1813 a vessel at Pin Mill "built for a stranger" was launched and ready to sail but was boarded by Customs Officers, who tried to detain her. But her crew, according to the *Ipswich Journal*, threatened to either throw them overboard or carry them over to Dunkirk.

The report goes on to say: — "The officers embraced the opportunity of a boat to go on shore, and left her in possession of the ruffians, who have made their escape with the vessel."

The builder, one Jonathan Godbold, stoutly denied that he "built fast cutters for strangers" and there being no evidence offered against him, the whole incident, and the cutter, was conveniently forgotten.

Another *Ipswich Journal* report, on 25th November, 1797, states briefly: — "42 half-ankers of geneva seized at Chelmondiston." And on 21st August 1830: — "This week 75 tubs of foreign brandy and geneva were seized . . . in a cave near the Cat House."

Strangely enough, the days of the Great Plague were a wonderful opportunity for smugglers. Sad-faced, sorrowing seamen came ashore with scores of hastily made coffins containing, they said, the bodies of their shipmates and passengers who had "died of the plague". Everyone on shore shrank away for fear of the dreaded infection and it was not for a long time that it was discovered by accident when a coffin was dropped and broken at

"All Clear" signal for the smuggler. Cat in the window of the Cathouse on the banks of the Orwell.

Manningtree, that the coffins were full of tubs of brandy, jars of gin and silks for my lady.

Many of the coffins were stacked openly in local churches and had actually had a burial service read over them by the clergy. Corpses used to be preserved in rum, as was Lord Nelson's after Trafalgar, so if the coffins gave off a strong odour of liquor the parson was easily satisfied. No doubt he would find a tub or two in his own cellar in due course. And he did *not* enquire how it had arrived there.

In the reign of Queen Elizabeth the First, one seventh of the entire British Fleet came from the Suffolk rivers. Even a little hamlet like Pin Mill had quite an array of fishing boats, barges and various types of coasting craft, many sailed by owner/skippers. Less than one hundred years ago there were thirty fishing boats, three spritsail barges, and two big coasting ketches, "boomies", owned in and around Pin Mill and Chelmondiston. The last Pin Mill-owned vessels were the fishing boat *Peace,* the late George Turner, the boomie barge *Sussex Belle*, the King family, and last of all, the coasting barge *Cambria*, owned and traded by myself until 1970. Now there is nothing but a host of little pleasure boats covering the anchorage from Butterman's Bay to Woolverstone, so that there is hardly room for a sizeable commercial vessel to go about her daily business, and certainly no place for her to anchor. Some yachts may be beautiful, but it is a complete change from days when the river scene consisted of barges, fishermen, schooners and square-rigged ships and the pubs were crowded with professional sailors.

Mrs Higgins, mother of the well known barge skipper "Mo" King, described to me how her father, Captain Garnham, told her one day to put on her best frock as they were going to launch a new barge at Ipswich. While she was upstairs she glanced into her parents' bedroom and saw a mass of golden sovereigns on the counterpane. These her father gathered up into a little leather bag. They were taken in the pony and trap to Bayley's shipyard at Bourne bridge, Ipswich, to pay for the barge. Mr Ralph Wilson, who was editor of the *East Anglian Daily Times*, kindly had the following extract reprinted for me.

"EAST ANGLIAN DAILY TIMES"
OF MARCH 6, 1884.

SHIP LAUNCH

On Tuesday was launched from the shipbuilding yard of Messrs. W. Bayley and Sons, St. Clement's, Ipswich, a new barge, boomsail rig, of about the following dimensions: Length 82ft. 8ins., breadth 19ft. 4ins., depth of side 6ft. 6ins. She is purchased by Mr. John Garnham, of Chelmondiston, and as she left the ways she was successfully christened by Miss Garnham the Blanche.

Mrs Higgins' Christian name was Blanche.

Captain Garnham was a well-known East Coast skipper, often bringing coal from the Tyne to Orford and Pin Mill. There were seven coal cargoes a year unloaded on Pin Mill Hard, down by the knoll posts, into horse wagons — four for the maltings, and three for the coal merchant who stowed it in what is now the *Butt* garage.

One day Captain Garnham took his wife and little daughter Blanche to sea, and his barge was overtaken by a terrible gale off Flamborough Head as she was bound north for the Tyne. For three days and nights she was under bare poles, washed fore and aft by wicked seas. Blanche and her mother lay in the cabin clasped in each other's arms and praying for deliverance. They fell asleep from sheer exhaustion. Let little Blanche, the late Mrs Higgins, take up the story in her own words: —

"The noise of the gale and the seas crashing over the decks made me think that our end was near and mother kept on praying and holding me tight. Then one morning I woke up and all was quiet. My mother was asleep. I ran up on deck and saw that the barge was in a quiet calm bay and looking ashore I saw turrets and a church tower rising up out of the early morning mist. The church bell was ringing and it all looked so peaceful and beautiful that I ran down to my mother and woke her saying 'Mummy, Mummy, your prayers have been answered. We've got to heaven'. I learned afterwards that my father had got the barge into the shelter of Robin Hood's Bay on the Yorkshire coast."

Pin Mill seamen had the reputation of being the best on this part of the coast. Names like Garnham, Lucas, Rands, Roberts, Strange, Quantrill and Burroughes were known from the Tyne to Cornwall.

Some ships which sailed from the Orwell in the 1830's were brought there by a gentleman who was styled "Emmigrant Agent", a Mr Samuel Noller of Debenham. He chartered the *Venus*, *Lochiel* and *Mary Stewart* to take hundreds of workhouse inmates to the New World. Each family was given five pounds to start a new life. These poor souls were brought in wagons to Redgate Hard above Freston and shipped away, never to see their native Suffolk again. Most went to Canada, some to New York and a few to British Honduras.

Local seamen have made themselves famous from the very earliest days of maritime history. Guerth the Saxon, who was held responsible for the defence of the Shotley peninsula, inflicted several sharp defeats on raiding Vikings. Once he lured them into the Orwell when King Alfred's warriors lay hidden behind the hill on which the Naval boys training establishment, H.M.S. *Ganges*, once stood. As the Vikings landed, King Alfred swept down on them while Guerth blocked their retreat with his local ships. There was such slaughter among the Danes that it was said both rivers, the Stour and the Orwell, ran red with their blood. From this battle, Shotley Spit, as we often call it now, gets its proper name, Bloody Point.

In Elizabethan times there was a famous navigator named Thomas Eldred, sailing out of the Orwell. He had a house in Fore Street, Ipswich. He acted as navigator to the famous Thomas Cavendish of Grimston Hall, Trimley—the second Englishman, after Drake, to circumnavigate the world.

Another famous seaman from the Orwell was Captain Broke of Broke Hall, Nacton. His house can be seen across the river from Pin Mill. He was so keen on joining the Navy as a lad that he used to paddle out into Butterman's Bay astride any log or plank he could find to try and go aboard the men-of-war lying there. The officers used to duly send him back home but when he continued this practice until the age of twelve, his father told the officers that they might as well keep him and take him away to sea, which they did. He became one of the greatest gunnery experts of his day.

His life's regret was that he missed Trafalgar; but he had some compensation when, in command of the frigate *Shannon*, he was sent to engage the crack American frigate *Chesapeake*, being refitted at Boston. The Americans had enjoyed two or three cheap victories over inferior British warships commanded by playboys and favourites from the Royal Court and the Admiralty thought it was high time a real seaman was sent out to teach the Americans a lesson. Broke from Nacton was just the man. Taking a few local seamen from the Orwell villages (mostly well known cut-throats and smugglers who were given temporary commissions for the purposes of boarding and hand-to-hand fighting!) and his expert gunners, trained at Devonport.

Broke sent a boat into the American port of Boston challenging the famous Captain James Lawrence to come out and fight. More than once the challenge had to be sent because Lawrence was perfecting every detail of his ship to be sure of notching another victory. A great banquet was prepared on shore because the salt-encrusted British frigate, smaller than the *Chesapeake*, was deemed a certain victim.

Out came the *Chesapeake*, pennants flying and her gilded rails sparkling in the sun. She looked a brave sight and the people of Boston came out in boats with bands playing to see the downfall of the *Shannon*. Broke kept his ship creeping along under lower topsails only, with a Trafalgar helmsman at the wheel. Under this sail the *Shannon* was almost upright and gave his trusted gunners steady aim.

The *Chesapeake* came surging up astern with all sails set and Lawrence thought he would be able to rake the *Shannon* from stern to stem. But with a slight shift of the wheel that weatherbeaten Trafalgar helmsman put the *Shannon* out of the line of fire and the *Chesapeake* had to luff to windward of her opponent. Broke gave orders to his master gunner, a man named Mindham, not to fire until the *Chesapeake*'s second gun-port was in his sights. Mindham held back until the critical moment. His shot was the signal for a devastating broadside which swept the American's decks, killing and maiming many in a matter of seconds and bringing the *Chesapeake's* fore-mast and yards crashing down on top of them.

The *Chesapeake*, her helmsman dead, flew up into the wind, was caught aback and blew stern on to collide with the *Shannon*. Broke's carpenter got his grapnels across and then lashed the two ships together so that Broke's Suffolk boarding party could get across. The carpenter lost his arm from a cutlass slash as he completed the knots.

Broke's men swarmed aboard, their captain in the van, and there was a brief and bloody encounter. Broke himself was attacked by four American seamen and received a terrible blow from a cutlass which almost scalped him. His men rushed to his aid and soon beat all the surviving Americans down below decks and battened them in.

The whole action was over in 15 minutes. This was the briefest and most famous ship-duel in naval history. The British flag was run up on the *Chesapeake's* signal halyard with the American flag below it to signify a British victory and the boatloads of onlookers could hardly believe the eyes as the little *Shannon* took the battered *Chesapeake* in tow and proceeded to sea, bound for Halifax.

Captain Broke was promoted to Admiral and came back to Nacton suffering badly from that terrible wound. Four years later he was found dying, holding his head, in the field behind Nacton beach opposite Pin Mill.

I have had the honour of having a drink in the replica of Broke's cabin built on to Broke Hall. The park gates were made from the *Shannon's* timbers.

Broke is commemorated in an old song which is still sung in Suffolk.

> The *Chesapeake* so bold
> sailed from Boston, we've been told
> to take a frigate neat and handy-o
> and the people of the port
> they came to see the sport
> and the bands were playing Yankee Doodle Dandy-o
> The British Frigate's name
> which for the purpose came
> to cool the Yankee courage neat and handy-o
> was the *Shannon*, Captain Broke
> and her crew were hearts of oak
> and at fighting were allowed to be the dandy-o
>
> The fight had scarce begun
> Before they flinched from their guns
> Which at first they started using neat and handy-o
> Then brave Broke he waved his sword
> And said 'Now, my lads aboard
> and we'll stop their playing Yankee Doodle Dandy-o'

We no sooner heard the word
than we quickly jumped aboard
and hauled down the Yankee colours neat and handy-o
And in spite of all their brag
Now the glorious British Flag
at the Yankee mizzen peak looks so handy-o

Here's a health brave Broke to you
to your officers and crew
who aboard the *Shannon* frigate fought so handy-o
and may it always prove
in fighting as in love
the British Tar will always be the dandy-o.

The new motor road sign for visiting yachtsmen.

CHAPTER THREE

Folk Lore

IT IS necessary to know Suffolk and Suffolk country folk over a very long period to sense the amazing thread of continuity which exists in the life of the county. Folk tales, occasionally in song, come down through the ages and are re-told without any emotion or amazement. One splendid old lady whose name was Wake "knew" her family were descended from Hereward the Wake:— "My great-great-grandfather knew that, and was proud of it," she told me. But this distinction was never boasted about because all the ruling classes and large landowners in East Anglia were of Norman descent, like the Gurdons who married into the Pretyman family of Orwell Park, and the Normans and Anglo-Saxons never did agree very well. Over at Helmingham the Tollemache family, whose history can be traced in the little village church, record that they were there "before the Normans came". This boast can still be read in memorials on the family caskets. When the Sutton Hoo ship was unearthed near Woodbridge, with its priceless treasures dating back to 600 A.D. (probably the property of Athelhere, an ancient King of East Anglia) an old inhabitant was asked if anyone round about ever suspected that the burial ship was underneath that mound. The answer was cautious, but he finally admitted "we always knew it was there". Asked how he knew, he said he couldn't recollect how he came to know. But his wife, who was much older, over ninety and a bit senile, nodded her bald head and muttered "The King's Ship".

*   *   *

Mr Rainbird Clarke, in his book on East Anglia, maintains that the people of the Ipswich area were originally the relatives and followers of the Royal Wuffings, from the royal house of Upsala, a few miles north of Stockholm. This does not mean that they were Swedish in the modern sense of the word, because the English, in their gradual migration westwards, once occupied that province before moving on into Schleswig-Holstein and thence to North Germany, Holland and Britain. They were the only people who practiced boat burials such as are found in Sweden and East Anglia. The sword, helmet and shield found in the ship were made in Sweden and were probably family heirlooms. The Wuffings ruled the Anglo-Saxon-Frisian population of Suffolk in the late fourth and fifth centuries. The name Wuffing seems to designate the family but each individual chief seems to be called Uffa or Offa and the great English leader is commemorated in such place names as Ufford, Uffington and Offton. His capital was Dunwich. The first Uffa of East Anglia, who came ashore in the region of Walberswick with the crews of six ships as the Romans departed, seems to have been a tremendously energetic person. He and his followers who came over shipload after shipload with women and children as well, cleared the forests, drained the low-lying land, established fords and bridges and linked up with resident Angles and Saxons who had for many years served as farm foremen and armed guards to wealthy Romans. No wonder the British chieftains invited them over to drive out the Picts and Scots who were ransacking and thieving homes and farms after the legions departed. The English were asked to come, so the Britons recorded, because they were "the most valiant race on the continent". Hengist and Horsa are the best known, and they certainly set about the Picts and Scots in such a manner that in a very short time there were none left in the south and east of the country. They were killed in fight or fled north and west.

The late Uffa Fox, the famous yacht designer of Cowes in the Isle of Wight, told me that his family originated in Suffolk. We used to meet at a boat show in London every year and have a few pints for old time's sake, for my father and I knew him long before he was famous. He always took care to remind me, "You should be bending the knee to me, Bob, for I am the last Uffa of East Anglia. There has always been an Uffa in our family and we are the true kings of East Anglia". This was generally after we had consumed several pints and gone on to tots of something stronger.

* * *

There is an age old difference between East Suffolk and West Suffolk. Under these names the county is nowadays divided into two separate councils — and they rarely agree. Traditionally what West Suffolk proposes East Suffolk opposes. There is more in this than meets the eye. A thousand years ago East Suffolk was inhabited by rip-roaring Danish Vikings and pirates, whereas in the hinterland were Anglo-Saxon farmers; solid, peaceful, hard-working and respectable Christians. They regarded with disgust and dismay, and some fear, their drunken fighting neighbours of the coastal areas. Go into a West Suffolk pub today and you will find a quiet atmosphere of friendliness and respectability. But in the East Suffolk coastal areas, where the wild North Sea governs people's lives to a large extent, you could have a riotous sing-song and dance and a punch on the nose for good measure any time you like. Things don't change! Old times, new times — they're all the same in Suffolk.

Suffolk dialect and forms of speech can be very difficult for the incoming stranger. Old Anglo-Saxon and ancient Danish words and pronunciation can still be detected by a sharp-eared listener well versed in these matters. The manner of expression is completely different from any other English dialect, and at times seems contradictory. A London yachtsman, asking an old Pin Mill seaman if he could let him have a barge's windlass handle for his houseboat was rather mystified to be told: "Dew I ain't I doubt I 'ont soon find one up." The prefix "do" pronounced "dew" is an order or instruction as in the old fisherman's song called "The Candlelight Fisherman": —

> Do you open the pane and pop out the flame
> to see how the wind do blow

Kessingland fisherman.

Of course, some Suffolk phraseology has caused strangers to mistake Selig Suffolk (meaning good and prosperous Suffolk) for Silly Suffolk. But there, as old Annie Powell of Pin Mill once said of a new bride in the village: — "She's a Londoner. *Very ignorant*." Or as another old worthy said of a nephew who had gone in for education: — "'Ere 'e come, with his head full of books and don't know a Brent Goose from a bloody Widgeon."

They knew geese from widgeon all right in the Suffolk villages, and how to catch hares with an old trawl net. First the feeding place of the hares was traced and then all the "runs", the worn hare tracks, would be blocked. Over the field gate was hung an old trawl net held in place by a few stones along the top bar. At the appropriate time, around dusk, one man would slowly walk round the field clapping his hands while his mate kept watch by the gate. The hare, disturbed by the clapping and finding all his usual runs blocked, would finally dash for the gate, going head first into the net and, bringing the stones down off the top bar, become hopelessly entangled. The gate-watcher did the rest.

There were once two brothers, skipper and mate of a small barge, who frequently replenished their grub locker in this manner. But one night the farm foreman and village policeman lay in wait for them, and just as the hare was collared in the net at the gate they dashed into the field and detained the clapper-out. Knowing him as a local character, they demanded the name of his partner who had, by then, beaten a hasty retreat into the night with the hare in his kit-bag.

"I ain't goin' to tell on 'im," said the stubborn old poacher. "You find out for yourself."

"If you tell us his name, it will make it better for you." Still he shook his head. "No, I ain't that sort of bloke. I ain't going to give away me own brother."

The trio then repaired to the local inn, where the hare had already been passed to an unknown destination and the brother was found having a quiet game of darts. Of course, evidence was given that he had "bin there all evenin'". And since no hare was found and much beer consumed, it was decided that there were no grounds for a charge and all went happily home to bed.

The old skipper remarked on the following Sunday morning, "There's nothin' like an old hare in the pot when you're layin' windbound at the Stone Heaps."

There is another story of an old East Anglian poacher who emerged through a gap in a farm hedge one night with a sack full of rabbits to find the local policeman waiting for him. "All right, fair cop," said the old fellow. "What now?"

"You'll have to bring them up to the police station. You've been taking them off private land."

So away they tramped across the fields and meadows, for it was a long way from the cluster of cottages on the hill. Soon the old man stopped and dumped the sack of rabbits on the grass.

"So these here rabbits ain't mine?" he said.

"That they ain't," said the policeman. "You got no right to 'em."

"Then if they ain't mine, I ain't goin' to carry 'em."

This attitude presented the Law with a bit of a problem. He needed the sack of rabbits for evidence and he would have to see them properly returned to the farmer. In the end, he took the only course possible, as far as he could see. He humped the heavy sack on his back, with the kind aid of the old poacher, and staggered along to the accompaniment of much puffing and blowing and resting to wipe his brow. Some of the water meadows were ankle deep in slush. At last, they came out onto the main road and had to pass by the poacher's cottage. Close to his gate, a suggestion was made that the policeman needed another rest, and down went the bag once more.

"'Ere, 'old on a moment," said the old poacher, removing his cap and running his finger round inside the grubby rim. "There's something I forgot," and after more fumbling he produced a half torn and greasy old piece of paper on which the writing was still readable. It was signed by the farmer, dated some six years previously, and gave permission to the bearer to trap, snare and shoot rabbits on his land.

The poacher and the policeman.

27

"I forgot all about this."

The policeman examined the document carefully under the light of his torch.

"Well," he said, "if this ain't never been revoked, you're in the clear."

"So these rabbits are mine, then?"

"Yes."

"Thank you very much, Officer," and picking up the sack, he pushed open his wicket gate and was soon indoors. Not every rabbiter has a policeman to carry his catch home over the fields.

Silly Suffolk? Did you say?

Making the film "Ha'penny Breeze" at Pin Mill in 1949.

CHAPTER FOUR

Fighting Suffolk

EAST Anglians have always been doughty fighters from earliest times. They bore the brunt of attacks by the ancient Vikings; marched to Hastings to form the nucleus of King Harold's army, jeering at villagers who had not the heart to join them on the way; brought the villainous King John to book at Bury St Edmunds; and formed the major part of Cromwell's New Model Army when two thousand of them routed the ten thousand Scots who were supporting the King. Suffolk peasants rebelled successfully against overbearing landowners and won battle honours under King George the Second at Dettingen. They also fought with distinction under Marlborough. The old Suffolk Regiment, now incorporated in the Royal East Anglian Regiment, were entitled to wear the Minden Rose commemorating their successes on the Continent.

In more recent times Suffolk folk stood firm for Marlborough's famous descendant, Sir Winston Churchill. During the Second World War against Hitler's Germany, Suffolk was really in the front line as Lowestoft Ness is the nearest point to Germany.

After this war the Suffolks distinguished themselves in Malaya, where they soon became adept at the jungle fighting necessary to put down a Communist rebellion. One Suffolk soldier told me:— "We was told to watch out for poisonous snakes with black and yellow stripes and to run yer hand up it and squeeze it abaft his head to kill it. My mate thought he see one and did as he were told. But he come back to base all blood and scratches somethin' terrible.

'What's happened?' I say to him.

He say 'You know the sergeant told us to run yer hand up them black and yellow snakes. Well, in the dark, I thought I saw one quite close to where I lay—so I done what the sergeant said and found me'self looking up a tiger's ass.'"

When the Suffolks came back from their successful campaign in Malaya they were given a tremendous welcome in Ipswich and Bury St Edmunds. Many honours and privileges were showered upon these sturdy sons of Suffolk.

Suffolk can well boast of its fighting men. The real Patron Saint of England is not a Czechoslovakian Knight of the Crusades named George who was almost unknown in England, but a Suffolk man, King Edmund. He was a devout Christian pacifist until the heathen Dane started to plunder and burn in his East Anglian kingdom. It is said that his pacifism was his downfall and the downfall of his people, for the barbaric Danes were not inclined to listen to the peaceful teachings of Christ. Too late, Edmund took up arms and harried the invaders wherever he could, from Ipswich and Bury St Edmunds to the coast. But finally he was overwhelmed and captured at a place called, in those days, Haegelisdun. There he was bound to a tree and shot to death with arrows because he would not renounce his faith and join the barbarians.

Hoxne claims to be the place where the deed was done, but many believe it was after a battle near Hollesley and that he was buried first at Sutton nearby. The old writers claim he was buried at Suthune, which may have been the old name for the place. Later the English monks were allowed to take his decapitated body to Bury St Edmunds. According to folk tales and legend a giant wolf was found guarding King Edmund's head in a Suffolk wood, after which it was miraculously joined to the body and the Saint as he was to become, was made whole.

Famous, or infamous, Suffolk warriors in Norman times were the Bigod family, who occupied at various times — and re-built at various times — the Castles of Framlingham and Orford. They were not true Suffolkers, being of Norman descent — harsh, defiant and independent. Their treatment of the local peasant folk was what one might expect of a cold-hearted conqueror.

Danish Vikings off the Suffolk Coast.

St Edmund — from a window in
Long Melford Church.

The Bigods were always mixed up in some sort of intrigue and rebellion
against anyone, from the king to their neighbouring barons, from the Conquest
down to King Henry the Second's reign. One of them, Hugh Bigod, allied
himself with the Earl of Leicester and fought against the King's troops at
Fornham All Saints. The sullen East Anglians would not fight for the hated
Bigod so he imported a small army of Flemings to fight for him. But the King's
men set about them with such slaughter that few escaped. In a small area of
Fornham All Saints a large number of skeletons have been unearthed, all with
cloven skulls and bones such as they would have suffered from the royal swords
and battle-axes.

All the Bigods, generation after generation, were much feared by the country folk because of their quick temper and warlike bearing. Somewhere in Bigod's Suffolk there is a path known locally as Bygott's Way, and it is not a place to wander about on dark and foggy nights. Some say the ghost of a Bigod rides along there at certain times of the year and heaven help any one in his way. The huge monster dog, Black Shuck, is said to have been seen on Bygott's Way near Bungay, where one of the Bigods had a castle. Even in these days nervous folk will tell you that they have actually seen this fearful dog-apparition, who seems to foretell the sort of disaster that either a fierce Bigod or the Devil himself might bring. Black Shuck is said to have appeared at a local church at the time of the Black Death. It is sad to think that one of Black Shuck's catastrophes is commemorated in the children's rhyme:

> Ring-a-Ring of Roses
> A pocket full of posies
> Atishoo Atishoo
> We all fall down.

The ring of roses was the ring of red blotches which marked the skin and the "posies" were carried by the victims to disguise the stench of the illness, and in the case of those still healthy, to act as a deterrent to infection. Finally, in a fever, he sneezed and fell down dead.

Black Shuck was "seen" in Suffolk during the bombing raids of the Second World War and the "sightings" are always linked with death and disaster. Perhaps he was trotting the woodland ways in June 1940, when Suffolk sailing barges put to sea from Ipswich to help rescue our soldiers, and some of their French allies, from Dunkirk. The *Barbara Jean* and the *Aidie*, owned by R. & W. Paul of Ipswich, sallied forth with stores for the troops retreating to the beaches under continuous air attacks by dive-bombers. The *Barbara Jean* had to be abandoned but her crew escaped. The *Aidie* was run up on to the beach with her cargo but a British Navy Officer in charge sent the crew aboard a destroyer and said the barge would have to be blown up. For some reason this was not done and the Germans took all her masts and sails out, repaired her, and used her later in the war as a store and coal hulk. Another Ipswich barge, the *Doris*, was blown up and the *Ena* abandoned. The *Ena* later returned, manned by soldiers, and arrived off Deal. She was later repaired at Ipswich and resumed trading.

The *Tollesbury* had better luck. It was a flat calm so the crew pushed the barge over the flats with setting booms, long poles, and took on board 200 soldiers. A destroyer came to her to take the men off but was called away to some more urgent action. Finally the crew got the barge off the beach and two destroyers tried to take the soldiers off, but both were sunk in the holocaust which was raging round the rescuing craft. At last a tug got a heavy wire fast

Dutch warships.

on the *Tollesbury's* windlass, went ahead at full speed, and pulled the windlass out of the deck. Captain Webb and his crew got another wire to the tug and this time everything held fast and she returned to England. The soldiers, who had been wading waist deep out to the *Tollesbury*, were full of praise for the gallant and untiring way the bargemen hauled them aboard in face of heavy fire and bombing. All the Suffolk bargemen got home safely.

There is little written in history books about a famous victory by Suffolk volunteers and country yokels over Holland's renowned Admiral de Ruyter. To tell you this story, well authenticated by the Admiralty Library, I must first recount how the Dutch Fleet came into the Thames Estuary and attacked the Kentish Medway before trying conclusions with Suffolk.

It was a peaceful June day in the Estuary over three hundred years ago when Admiral de Ruyter, with seventy-one fighting ships, came standing across the Sunk Head close hauled on the port tack to take the last of the flood into the King's Channel. The wind was light from the south west and as the ebb came away they leisurely clewed up and came to anchor off the Gunfleet sand. What a sight they must have been to local vessels hugging the shore, and to watchers standing on the high ground above Felixstowe, Walton-on-the-Naze and Frinton. They had been seen from Kent, too, and soon identified. This was a great hostile fleet, utterly unexpected, and nowhere had preparations been made to meet any such attack. After years and years of war against the Spanish, French and Dutch, apart from the miseries of England's own Civil War everyone had thought that an era of peace was at hand. English plenipotentiaries were ever on the Continent negotiating a general European settlement to be called the Peace of Breda. The corrupt, pleasure-loving King Charles II had ordered the British Fleet to be laid up and promptly appropriated for his own extravagances some two million pounds which should have been used to pay the seamen, and provide for their food, stores and ammunition. All repairs to English warships were stopped and the largest vessels laid up in the Medway. Admiralty officials mostly promoted for court reasons rather than for any knowledge of the sea, took their line of behaviour from the King and right down through the shore establishment funds intended for ships and seamen were embezzled right, left and centre. Arthur Tedder, B.A., author of *The Navy of the Restoration*, refers to "Sturdy, willing seamen become paupers, diseased and mutinous; volunteers became deserters; fine old sea Captains displaced by foppish courtier ignoramuses who often as not owed their preferment to disreputable intrigue in a disreputable court; lack of food; bad food; lack of pay and pensions; State money, stores and prizes embezzled by men of every rank . . ."

No wonder de Ruyter thought it safe to bring his fleet into the Thames Estuary in spite of the fact that it had been internationally acknowledged that the English had won command of the sea. His reason was to "do a Pearl

Harbour". His plan was almost a blueprint for the Japanese to follow against the United States Fleet two hundred and seventy-four years later. While the peace negotiations dragged on he would strike a blow that would make him master of the sea, or at least enforce better terms from the British. The wind being south west, it was at first thought that he would attack Harwich, where there was considerable shipping laid up, though mainly merchantmen. But that night the wind backed to the east-south-east and freshened. This was a bit of luck for the Dutchmen as they now had a fair wind to the Medway. They weighed immediately and sailed up to the Nore Buoy. De Ruyter sent Lieutenant Admiral van Ghent up Sea Reach with a light squadron to capture or destroy ten frigates and twenty ships lying in and just below the Lower Hope, but these withdrew to Tilbury to go under the protection of the fort there. It being high water by then, van Ghent thought discretion the better part of valour and beat back to the Nore while the ebb served him. The ships he had hoped to capture were in fact convict ships and their escorts "in the Barbados trade". Perhaps the Dutch thought they could free the convicts and use them to fight against the British Fleet.

Now the great attack on the Medway began. Sheerness Fort was bombarded for one and a quarter hours, with very little reply. The scanty defenders had hardly any ammunition. Then 800 Dutch soldiers landed and took over the Fort, led by an Englishman named Captain Dolman, a renegade Republican. There was a brief and spirited resistance from a small body of men under Sir Edward Spragg, but he was forced to withdraw along the river bank.

The whole Dutch Fleet now made sail, the wind having freshened from the north east, and sailed up the Medway. A protective boom in the form of a chain had been laid across the river, somewhat hastily, but it was not properly made fast and gave way at the impact of the first ship. Up they swept, fireships and all, and all poor old Spragg could do was to follow them along the south bank and blaze away with a few muskets whenever they came within his range. His was a gallant effort but quite useless to stop a fleet of this magnitude.

One or two British war ships, almost crewless, banged away for a few minutes at the Dutch but were soon either sunk or set on fire. Up river there was little short of panic. The largest of the laid up warships were towed and hauled up above the second chain boom which was stretched across just above Upnor Fort and it was here that the Dutch met with the hottest fire and many of their men were killed. With a fair wind and flood tide and all sail set, two ships charged the boom. The first one failed to break it but the second, surging up almost on top of her at great speed, caused the supporting dolphins to tumble and the chain, with the weight of the two ships on it, parted.

De Ruyter, in spite of his sixty years, now jumped into a rowing boat and was pulled this way and that directing operations, pointing out which ships were the most valuable, which were to be sunk or set on fire, and which ones to capture if possible. Off Chatham, de Ruyter found four of the pick of the British Navy—the famous *Royal Charles* (82 guns), *Saint James* (82 guns) *Loyal London* (90 guns) and *Royal Oak* (76 guns). All were unmanned. Fireships were brought up and placed alongside *Saint James, Loyal London* and *Royal Oak* and they were soon enveloped in smoke and flames, the crackling roar of their death throes adding to the awesome noise of gunfire and musketry.

In the meantime Dutch seamen boarded the *Royal Charles*, cut her cables and, it now being after high water, let her drive down river until they could take her in tow by one of their ships. At first she grounded, being a deep draught ship, but working like demons the Dutchmen threw everything they could to one side of the ship to give her a heavy list and thus make her draw less water. Thus they got her away and eventually towed her across to Holland. They also picked up the smaller *Unity* and took her as well.

In the meantime Dutch troops landed at Gillingham to forage for food, but, under strict instructions from the Admiral, behaved in exemplary fashion towards the population, paying for what they had and doing no harm to any house or person. De Ruyter said that, above all things, he did not want to "anger the English nation by spoiling and burning" as this would bring them about his ears like hornets and that was something he did not wish to contemplate. They would unite against him and never agree to the terms the Dutch wanted at the Peace Conference.

De Ruyter might have forced the action even further up the Medway but news came to him that the redoubtable General Monck, the Duke of Albemarle, had drawn several thousand seasoned troops across Rochester Bridge and on both banks of the river. These the Dutch commanders did not care to tackle. Later de Ruyter sternly reprimanded them for their lack of spirit in this respect.

That night, the action over, the Dutch fleet anchored in the river off Hoo. It is said that English pilots from Hoo accepted money to pilot them out of the river and a number of half-starved and poverty-stricken English seamen swam out to the Dutch ships and offered their services. They were paid money in advance and signed on, the first real money some of them had had for nearly two years. Up to then they had been given I.O.U. tickets which eventually the local shopkeepers refused to accept as the Admiralty had not honoured them.

Thus the raid ended and the invaders sailed away with the south east wind towards Orfordness.

Now what he had done in Kent, de Ruyter thought he could do in Suffolk. But while he was lambasting the Kentishmen, Harwich seamen had drawn old colliers across the narrow entrance of what was then called Orwell Haven and sunk them as the Dutch Fleet approached, completely blocking the harbour. De Ruyter adopted the ruse of sailing down past Orfordness as if bound to attack further north—then coming about and fetching back to Felixstowe. But silly Suffolk was not to be caught napping. Local merchant skippers and pilots knew that with the wind in the south-east no Dutch commander, however daring, would allow his ships to become bottled up in the swift tides of such narrow creeks as the Alde, the Blyth, or Lowestoft, where in those days the harbour was only a tidal inlet. So the Governor of Landguard Fort, off Felixstowe, Captain Nathanial Darrell, had troops marched from Sudbury, Aldeburgh, Southwold, Dunwich and Lowestoft to reinforce the small garrison he had in the Fort.

It was on 2nd July at seven a.m. that the Dutch fleet was seen rounding Orfordness with the ebb, only to come about off Aldeburgh as the flood tide made, arriving off the Deben by 11 a.m. De Ruyter had five ships anchored in the Sledway Channel as a guard against any surprise from a light British squadron which was at that time cruising off the north-east coast. But with the wind south-east they had no hopes of getting to the southward and in any case may have been unaware of the Dutch attack.

Another nine ships were sent to the Rolling Ground off Harwich to bombard the Fort; and forty-seven ships, many of them carrying troops, anchored off what is nowadays the east end of Felixstowe promenade. By this time there was very little wind, almost a calm. In fact the ships sent to the Rolling Ground had difficulty in getting near Landguard and much of their bombardment fell short.

Now the great assault commenced. Some three thousand Dutch soldiers, again led by the renegade Captain Dolman, swarmed ashore on Felixstowe beach and tried to storm the Fort from the land side. But no sooner did they rear up their scaling ladders than Darrell's men tipped them over or drew them up with boat-hooks and hitchers. Darrell was a Man of Kent from a village near Ashford and I understand his family still retain one of the Dutch scaling ladders as a souvenir.

The gallant English commander, short of ammunition, thanks to the money having been appropriated by Charles, his Court and his Ministers, ordered his cannon to fire into the shingle just ahead of the advancing Dutch to send up a shower of pebbles and giving the enemy the impression that he had numerous and well supplied musketeers. Many a bold Dutchman fell with a pebble between the eyes. Those that reached the walls of the Fort were treated to a well-aimed fusillade and not a single Dutchman got inside the defences. Captain Darrell was wounded by a ball in the shoulder, but not dangerously, and he continued to direct operations until the entire assault force had been driven back along Felixstowe beach. It was a Dutch disaster. To add to their troubles, the Earl of Suffolk brought up his "trained bands" from the countryside roundabout and gained the high ground on Felixstowe cliff. Composed of country chaps who could pot a hare or a pheasant on a dark night, poachers, gamekeepers and the like—not to mention gangs of smugglers, they found that a Dutch soldier was an easy target. The Earl of Suffolk's men may not have been disciplined soldiers but one thing they could do was to shoot straight without wasting ammunition.

All the Dutch could do was to scramble for their boats and haul them off the beach. There was apparently some disorder in this operation as they were late on the tide and the ebb had left some of them high and dry. More Dutchmen died as they tried to drag them off and some of the boats had to be loaded with dead and wounded. Many of the boats drove straight down towards Shingle Street on the ebb and were ordered to try and make a landing in Hollesley Bay; but with the tide pouring out of Orford Haven and a few more fusillades from a small "trained band" stationed at Orford, who had moved down to the shore, not a single boatload gained the shore and they had to return to their ships. As de Ruyter's great fleet hauled on the wind and headed seawards you can imagine the Suffolk yokels whooping and shouting "That'll larn 'em".

Dutch Admirals de Ruyter, van Tromp and Opdam, had good cause to remember the Suffolk coast. Some 300 years ago the land-folk lined the high ground and watched great fleets locked in thunderous battle; once when the English and Dutch fought a "draw" in Sole Bay; and on another occasion when Prince Rupert's ships came sweeping round Orfordness to attack a six-mile long line of Dutchmen and smashed the Hollanders into a terrible defeat. A contemporary report says that Prince Rupert charged the Dutch line like a troop of cavalry. The sea off Orfordness was "filled with splendid ships of the line under clouds of canvas".

The dashing cavalier Prince must have been a formidable opponent on land or sea. Horseback or shipboard, his one aim in war was to get to grips with the enemy as quickly as possible, and even in defeat his only thought was to get back into the fight.

CHAPTER FIVE

The Great Flood

THE old faces of parts of Suffolk have to some extent been preserved and recorded by Preservation Societies, whose devoted members are, I fear, constantly fighting a losing battle against people called "developers" who have already altered the entire character of the district and the people. Who cares now that "Edwardus Rex Anglia" (1315) was Lord of the Manor of Chylminton (Chelmondiston) and Woolfterton (Woolverstone and Pin Mill)?

As a matter of interest I have listed the other local Lords of Manors in this district, The Hundred of Samford, in the year 1315, and here they are: —

Kyrketon	—	Wittus Vicedelue
Herkested	—	Wittus le Bretoun
Statton	—	Wittus Vicedelue
Bergholt	—	Pnus de Orebye
Heigham	—	John de Reynes
Roydon	—	Robtus de Roydon
Capell	—	Wittus filius Radi
Belsted	—	Abbas de Albermalia
Tatingston	—	John Holbrook
Freeston	—	{ John de Holbrook { John de Freston
Belsted	—	John de Goldingham
Hintlesham	—	{ John Talbot { Margeria Pypard
Erwarton	—	Barthus Davilliers
Holbrook	—	John de Holbrook
Brantham	—	Wittus de Brantham
Stratford	—	John de Stratford
Shelley	—	John de Applebye
Wenham	—	Petronella de Holbrook
Holton	—	Wittus de Boyton
Bentley	—	Hugo Tollemache
Whersted	—	Robtus de Roydon
Corpedocke	—	Richus de Corpedocke
Chylminton } Woolfterton }	—	Edwardus Rex Anglia
Sproughton	—	Wittus de Ormesbye

In those days, and for long after, the fishing weirs were rented from the Lord of the Manor and a name which has come down through the centuries is Colin's Weir in the Orwell, now called Collimer Point at the lower end of Butterman's Bay, and there is a port hand light buoy there now named Collimer. There were also many oyster beds and salt-pans along the river bank. Another bend in the river is called Potter Point, opposite Pin Mill and this may have been named either from a pottery situated at the back of the *Butt and Oyster* or after the large local family named Potter, who lived in the district some four hundred years ago. In 1556 there was a brewer in Ipswich named Potter and his daughter, Anne, was burned as a martyr to her religion at the Cornhill.

Big tides, helped by north west gales, often flooded over the banks of the river, but as far as is known there was none so disastrous as the one we experienced on 31st January 1953. I was talking to an old shipmate in front of my cottage fire that night when at 10 o'clock we heard a north-wester come howling through the trees.

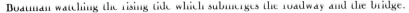

Boatman watching the rising tide which submerges the roadway and the bridge.

"There's going to be a big tide tonight, Bill," I said. "I'll go down to the Butt and shift my old car. It's high water at 2.15 in the morning."

We were too late to think about car shifting. It was already half-submerged and the tide was rushing up the path past the gates of the cottages and into their gardens and houses. And it was not yet half flood! Everyone rushed to help the widows and old people take their furniture upstairs but generally speaking the roaring tide and battering wind beat us and everyone lost their heavy pieces. By high water it was up seven stairs in my cottage, five feet deep in the front room and the top of the garden gate just visible. The gale blew at a hundred miles an hour nearly all night, and it was bitterly cold. Farm land and gardens were ruined for the season by the salt water. In the morning there were yachts and boats in people's gardens lying at crazy angles. The boat builders' "office", an old wooden railway carriage, was smashed to pieces. All his bills, books and business papers were strewn over the meadows mixed up with the contents of chemical lavatories, and a fine old job he and his lads had sorting one bit of paper from another. Old Ephraim took the most philosophical view of it all in the morning.

"People make a lot of fuss over a bit of water," he said. "All I lost was that old settee and I never could get to sleep on it so I sawed it up and put it on the fire to dry the house out. Then the old woman says 'Where's the lavatory

Big tide at Pin Mill.

bucket, Ephraim' — and there it was over by the stile all washed out and ready for use."

By way of contrast, on the anniversary of this disaster we had the lowest tide ever recorded, and the river shrunk to a mere stone's throw from bank to bank. We had a commemoration service in the *Butt and Oyster*.

A lesser known event in the village was an attempt to kidnap Lord Nuffield. A small yacht arrived at the anchorage and George Burroughes, who was then harbour master, was asked for a mooring and for some reason he took a dislike to the gentlemen concerned and mentioned this to P.C. Mann, who was the local constable at the time. For no real reason, George suspected they were "up to no good". It was at the time when Lord Nuffield was purchasing the Woolverstone and Orwell Estates as gifts to Oxford and Cambridge Universities.

The wires hummed and plain clothes policemen dashed between Pin Mill and London. Soon it was discovered that his Lordship was to be kidnapped from his bed in London, brought to Pin Mill, put aboard the yacht, taken out to sea and held to ransom. Detectives hid in Lord Nuffield's bedroom and when the intending kidnappers broke in, they were promptly arrested. An aerial view of Pin Mill even appeared in *The Times*.

In the meantime, P.C. Mann had orders to keep guard on the yacht. George put him aboard and left him there, to Mr Mann's considerable apprehension as he hated being on the water. It is said that, as soon as it was known in the village that P.C. Mann was stuck aboard the yacht with no means of getting ashore, there were more pheasants poached than on any other night of the year.

Now little old seafaring Pin Mill has passed into history, except for the ancient *Butt and Oyster Inn*. Perhaps the only event of note in recent years was when my barge *Cambria*, the last genuine trader under sail, was called up to Ipswich by the malsters, Pauls and Whites Limited. We were asked to carry a large export order of malt to an ocean-going ship in London, every available power vessel had been chartered and some had been held up by bad weather. Taking a chance the firm asked me to load the *Cambria* and rush the last load to London under sail in time to catch the ship on her last day in the dock. *Cambria* with every stitch set to a north west breeze made it in time, saving the

The author's barge *Cambria* trying out her racing sails in 1955. Note the two sheeted jib on the bowsprit.

Cabin of the *Cambria*.

Tower Bridge opening for the Pin Mill barge *Cambria* in 1964. She finished trading in 1970 and was taken over by the Maritime Trust as a Museum.

merchants concerned considerable financial loss. Lloyds of London thought fit to mention her kindly in their worldwide press.

Barge is chartered for export order

THE "Cambria", the last engineless commercial sailing barge in commission, has been unexpectedly chartered so that a British company can meet an urgent export order.

She is due to leave Ipswich dock this evening for London with 100 tons of malt consigned to Kenya.

Shipping congestion in London has delayed the turn round of the five motor barges owned by Pauls and Whites Ltd., the Ipswich based £12 million animal feeding stuffs and maltings group, and it was essential that the malt should arrive in London for transhipment to the ss Clan Malcolm which is sailing soon for Mombasa.

To meet the delivery date, the company has chartered the "Cambria", owned by Capt. Bob Roberts, of Pin Mill, who is sailing her to the King George V Dock, London, where she is expected to arrive on Monday afternoon.

Barge *Cambria* owned and skippered by the author. Pin Mill.

CHAPTER SIX

Barge Hounds and Suffolk Lurchers

"A REAL, genuine Suffolk barge hound . . . that's what he is," Bill Kemble told me when his barge was at Cliff Quay, Ipswich. "D'you know, I once took that dawg to London with me in the barge because my missus wanted to go and stay with her mother for a day or two. Mostly the old dawg stayed at home with her. And blow me if I don't go and lose him at the Surrey Dock. Couldn't find him nowhere. And that there hound, believe it or not, walked all the way back to Ipswich on his own. Found his own way from Surrey Dock back here to Ipswich."

Well, I **did** believe it at the time, as I am sure Bill Kemble did. In fact he died in this belief, because it was not until several years after that I heard the whole story of this remarkable animal . . . this genuine Suffolk barge hound; although he looked just a long-legged nondescript mongrel to me.

This is what really happened. There were two sailing barges under the same ownership trading between Ipswich and London and they were sister ships. Bill Kemble had one (the faster one by all accounts) and the other was skippered by a relative, Jack Kemble; and they were very far from being good friends. Always they had been sailing rivals and time and again they had sailed against each other to be first back to Ipswich.

Jack was tired of being beaten by the faster barge and the time had come to resort to intrigue. He could never beat her barge for barge.

They were both loaded with cattle cake and ready for sea. Both hove down to the lock gates ready to go out. On board with Bill was this genuine Suffolk barge hound, the darling of his wife's heart. "She thinks more of that ole dawg than she do of me," he used to say. Bill had been specially enjoined to look after the dog **above all else**. And Jack knew that.

There was an hour or so to wait for the high water lock-out so Bill and his mate went below to have their dinner. The genuine Suffolk barge hound was left sprawling on an old sack on the main hatch. Presently the dog smelt something tempting. It was a large and meaty bone shoved under his nose by the mate of the rival barge. The bone was withdrawn quietly to the side of the barge and eventually up on to the quay. The hound eagerly followed and found himself aboard the other barge. Then suddenly he was seized by a pair of horny hands and precipitated down the forecastle hatch, complete with

Barge dog on watch.

meaty bone there to feast himself in darkness with the scuttle hatch tightly shut.

Soon came the cry of the lock foreman. "Sailorman, ahoy. You ready? Come ahead."

Jack and his mate smartly hove their barge into the lock but the other barge did not follow. In reply to a repeated "Come on", and "What's the matter? We can't wait all day", Bill Kemble came along the quay and said; "I've lorst me little old dawg. He was aboard a minute ago. Give us a few minutes to find him, will you?"

"Well, hurry up," the lockman said and Bill and his mate went off along the quay, whistling and calling round the warehouses—but not a sign of the genuine Suffolk barge hound did they see.

At last the lockman could wait no longer. It was gone high water and there were other craft waiting outside to come in. He locked Jack Kemble's barge out but Bill's remained in the dock. It was more than his married life was worth to sail for home without that dog. He and his mate scoured the entire

Surrey Dock system from Rotherhithe nearly down to Greenwich. They whistled, they shouted, they called. But no response, no dog.

In the meantime, with the favouring westerly breeze, Jack Kemble and his mate were setting their sails and bowling down Limehouse Reach counting the hours when they would be tied up in Ipswich, which would be the next day.

For three days, Bill stayed in the dock. He asked the police. He asked the P.L.A.* staff to help. He even asked the dockers. Until, at last, despondent, he locked out and sailed for Ipswich — minus the Suffolk barge hound. Next day he arrived at Ipswich just as his rival had finished unloading and was coming away for London again. He pretended not to hear their jibes.

"Where you been — fishing?" and lots of other caustic comments as well. He slung his kit-bag over his shoulder and walked up through the town to the cottage where he lived.

Then the storm broke.

Sitting outside his front door was the genuine Suffolk barge hound. And in the doorway was his missus with a face like thunder.

"You may well come home, Bill Kemble. Don't tell me no lies. I know where you've been. You've been down in that pub with your cronies swilling beer. I know you got into the Quay three days ago 'cos the dog came on up home but you hadn't got the decency to come with him. When he come in the door, I got your dinner ready an'all, but you can go back aboard your barge to eat for all I care. Your dinner's in the dustbin."

Bill stood there flabbergasted and couldn't get a word out. Poor Bill. Jack had beaten him to the Quay and now he'd ran slap into this squall from his missus. But still he marvelled how that dog could have found his way all that

*P.L.A. — Port of London Authority.

48

distance from the Surrey Dock to his home in Ipswich. It's a tidy step. Close on fifty miles and through the London traffic and all. Bill told the tale on and off to his dying day, that a real Suffolk barge hound will always find his way to Ipswich.

But Jack never breathed a word until long after Bill's death. Then he came out with the whole story in the *Nelson* at Ipswich. "No sooner did my barge touch Ipswich Quay," he said, "than that little old dawg recognised where he was and was off home as quick as his legs could carry him. But we beat old Bill's barge proper that time. I reckon we'll have another pint on the old dawg."

Sailing barges often had dogs aboard. One skipper known as "Monkey" Gray, trained a giant Alsatian to keep thieves and vagabonds off his deck. The dog was a very fierce and efficient watchkeeper, but one dark night failed to recognise his master's voice, coming alongside in a small boat. The skipper was drunk and incoherent and the dog refused to have this strange voice aboard, snarling and snapping at the hand which attempted to clutch the rail. The skipper had to retreat and scull back ashore to plead for a "kip" on the pub bench until morning.

When I was coasting in the barge *Cambria* I had an old lurcher called Dusty who would bark at buoys in a thick fog long before the mate and I could see them.

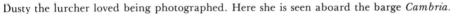

Dusty the lurcher loved being photographed. Here she is seen aboard the barge *Cambria*.

When Dusty was ashore, I used to take her over to Gedgrave marshes near Orford where my old friend, John Seymour, the author of many excellent country books, had a small holding. John owned a long-legged lurcher named Esau. At one time he had two lurchers, a smooth coated one named Jacob and this rough haired one called Esau. John was a great one at naming his animals. His two pigs were called Sodom and Gomorrah.

Esau was incredibly fast and he and Dusty used to hunt hares like well trained partners. Dusty, who had the best nose, would smell out a hare and start it but was never quite fast enough to overtake. Esau would lie patiently, belly down in the grass, and take up the chase as Dusty began to lose ground and Esau never failed to take his quarry.

One day, a local squire rang up John, saying, "That blasted dog of yours is over on my land chasing hares." To which John replied, "You must be mistaken. The dog is here sitting beside me now."

"But I saw him here only two minutes ago."

Of course John could afford to smile. True, the dog was sitting beside him; but he did not reveal to the irate squire that it only took the speedy Esau two minutes to cover the mile between the estate and John's cottage.

Many years ago, "Dot" Quantrill at Pin Mill had a fine old lurcher who would trot behind his bike round the lanes. When "Dot" came to a likely place for game he would send the dog into the woods and and then ride on for a mile or so. And the cunning old lurcher, maybe with a pheasant or partridge in his mouth, would not come out on to the road until "Dot" rang his bicycle bell—the "all clear" signal.

"Dot" was never short of a meal for his family and never once was he caught trespassing. He had a small fishing boat, not only for catching fish, but also to collar the odd pheasant off the sea wall on a cold dawn. When the ice and frost were on the birds' backs and wings they would not take off and were easy prey for the likes of "Dot" . . . and his lurcher.

When John Seymour moved across to a farm in Wales, I paid him a visit and picked up from his neighbour a border collie pup, only five weeks old. It was a bitch and the parents were fine working sheepdogs. When I got back to Suffolk with this amusing and highly intelligent little creature, I took her into a lonely riverside pub where I met a local farm hand who was a "sheepminder", a grade below a real shepherd.

"What do you think of my new dog, Brom?" I asked.

"Ah," he said, "that's a good dog. That'll grow into a good 'un. You know, years ago, I had one of them, black and white just like yourn—old Jess. She was the best little old dawg I ever had. She'd fetch for me—fetch anything. If I had a spring lamb get adrift, I'd just tell old Jess and she'd go scouting round and fetch her back in no time. Do you know, one day we put an old ram in to the ewes and he was a bit wild and frisky and jumped the gate and ran down along the road. 'Jess,' I said, 'go and fetch that old ram — and she come back with our Rector.'"

Old Brom often told this tale about his bitch Jess. Actually, the rector, who had long been suspected of being a bit of a lady killer, and was very popular among both young and old of the fair sex, had seen Brom's dog out along the road and fearing it would get run over, called it to him. Seeing it was Brom's sheepdog, he pedalled slowly along to the meadow where he knew Brom had his sheep, the dog trotting obediently along behind the parson's bicycle. Pausing for a kindly word with the old sheepminder, the holy man little suspected that he was perpetuating a taproom tale that would live for many years to come.

Barge dog at work.

CHAPTER SEVEN

Suffolk Humour

THERE is deep and natural humour among Suffolk men, slow and
meaningful, and couched in the terms of an age gone by. None of the
quick repartee of the Cockney or the roaring ribaldry of the northern shires. A
solemn face, a slow smile, and often the joke will hang fire for generations.
Dear old Cully Tovell, a coasting barge master for most of his eighty-five years,
once said of his somewhat unsatisfactory mate:— "Slow?—He's too slow to
carry a cold dinner to a corpse; but he's got enough mouth for another row of
teeth." Some of Cully's old sayings and similes, which could hardly bear the
publicity of cold print, will live on for many a year.

When George Turner's old fishing smack, the *Peace*, was put on the posts
for much needed repair, Ted Webb, the shipwright, shook his head sadly and
commented, "She's getting old, George. I can't make a new boat of her."

"I don't want you to make a new boat of her, Ted. I just want you to make
sure she can go on getting older and older."

"Coddy" Polly, all the numerous Polly tribe were called Coddy, once
came into the *Butt and Oyster* and told us he had signed on a Negro mate.

"Black as the ace of spades, he is. Never seen such a black'un. If you
rubbed a bit of coal on his cheek, that would leave a white mark."

I must tell you the story of Coddy's brother, Mick—Mick Coddy—as far as
possible, in his own words of how he first went to sea in a barge at the age of
twelve. He had walked from Harkstead to Pin Mill Hard, where a boomie barge
was being got ready for a voyage to the Tyne to load coal for Pin Mill Maltings.
He asked the mate for a job and was immediately taken on at half a crown a
week.

"I ran nearly all the way back home. 'Mother,' I said, 'I've got a job in a
barge'. I knew she'd be pleased because there were so many of us to feed that
on Sundays she used to make a bloody great duff in the wash tub to keep our
bellies full. 'Well done, Mick boy,' she says, 'I can't give you much to start off
with but here's a shilling and God bless you.' So I sailed away with mother's
shilling; and oh dear, was I sick. I felt like dying and every time I washed the
dishes I bust several cups and plates and the skipper said he would make me
pay for everything I broke and would knock it off my wages. Well, what with
me going ashore for a bottle of ginger pop and some grub in Newcastle, and
then breaking some lamp glasses on the voyage back—when I paid off at Pin

Old hands watch for a nor'wester which means a swollen tide.

Mill and the deductions for breakages had been made — I'd been away a fortnight — I had eightpence to come! I'd started off with a shilling." Such was life before the First World War.

An old couple from West Suffolk once ventured into Norfolk to visit relations. On the local railway the good wife wanted to make sure she did not sit with her back to the engine so her husband made the necessary enquiries of the guard and came back to the carriage with the needed information.

"Now do you set there, my dear, and I'll set opposite with my back to the engine."

At Norwich the train did an about turn and an engine was put on the other end to complete the journey so that the wife had her back to the engine.

Mystified, the old chap remarked: — "That's a rum'n. When we started I was settin' opposite you and now you're settin' opposite me."

One day, two old Pin Millers were sitting on the old wooden seat at the top of the hard when a particularly attractive and scantily dressed young yacht lady went tripping down to a waiting dinghy. The old pair regarded this beautiful apparition solemnly until she disappeared on board a smart yacht on the moorings. Old George's comment was, "If I'd known as much when I was young as I know now, I'd 'ave 'ad more than I did 'ave."

"Ah," replied Percy, slowly shaking his head, "and cheaper, too."

An American yachtsman on a deep sea cruise took an overland trip to Sudbury where he found and bought the very musical instrument he had for years been looking for, a genuine old virginal. It was housed in a handsome old box and he wanted a waterproof canvas cover for it. Jack Powell, the sailmaker, was sent for and he waddled across to the shipwright's shed with his tape measure and then regarded the box with some curiosity.

"What is it," he asked the American.

In a slow Texan drawl, the visitor proudly exclaimed, "That's a genuine virginal."

Still mystified, Jack regarded it a little longer and then his blue eyes twinkled as he gave me a nudge: "It ain't the sort we know, is it Bob?"

Tales of Suffolk humour could fill a book, such as the village bus driver who grumbled about there being so many little humped back bridges: "And they stuck 'em all in the middle of the road". And the Shotley farm hand, directing a lost motorist, starting off his explanation of the intricate lanes, "'Well, if I wanted to go to Holbrook, I shouldn't start from here."

Grim, deep and longlasting—and may the Suffolk rural dweller never forsake his native humour in spite of the influx of "foreigners" in recent years.

Talking about foreigners, I once asked the late Miss Annie Powell, the sailmaker's sister, when she was over eighty years of age, how many genuine old Pin Millers were still living in the village. She could recount but a few and I mentioned the name of my neighbour, Bill Simpson. He was born in Lark Cottage and had lived there all his life and was to become the oldest local inhabitant.

Bargeman's tune-up in the *Butt and Oyster Inn*.

"Bill Simpson," bridled Miss Powell, "he ain't a Pin Miller, his father came from Shotley."

That was three and a half miles away!

Of course, Pin Mill always had a "Mayor". At one time it was a local greengrocer who lived close to the *Butt and Oyster*. Then the chain of office fell to Hazeal Booth, a barge hand and boatman, and it was during his term of office that local cottagers built a little wooden bridge over the Grindle, the little stream which runs by a row of cottages across the common. Of course, there had to be an opening ceremony. To the firing of shotguns and music on my old melodeon, the Mayor was brought out of the *Butt* seated in an old armchair mounted on a four-wheeled barrow. Cutting the tape with his clasp knife, he pronounced the bridge open and inscribed the date in the still soft cement, impressing therein several beer bottle tops to help mark the occasion. All hands then retired to the *Butt* to song and dance led by George Burroughes, the harbour master.

The next Mayor was Ephraim Sharman, a fine old local character and a real bit of old Suffolk. All his young life he had been a sailorman in the local barges and his son and grandson followed suit. Ephraim had a cocked hat made for him with port and starboard lights on it, a gown filched from some unsuspecting schoolmaster, and a chain of office complete with swivel which had at one time served as a yacht mooring in the River Orwell. At every local celebration or sing song, he went round with the Royal National Life-boat Institution box and, with the help of Bill Simpson, collected such a record sum that an official from London made a special visit to the *Butt* to congratulate them and stand them a dinner.

In 1978 Mayor Ephraim was over eighty years of age, but his grandson, Peter, who was at sea with me in the barge *Cambria* when he was very young, was trading between the East Coast and the continent in a small motor barge. Peter has inherited all the old humour from his ancestors, one of whom fought in the *Victory* at Trafalgar and supported Lord Nelson's head and shoulders as he was being carried below after being shot. The Sharman of those days demanded it as his right and duty to a fellow East Anglian.

Peter, at the age of ten, was once accosted by two city hikers who asked: — "If we follow that path up the hill, where do we come out?" Peter regarded them solemnly for a moment and his answer was a bit of classic Suffolk. "You come out on top."

When they muttered something about "Silly Suffolk", he went to grandfather Ephraim, who was tending a boat close by and said: — "Grandad, them people called my Silly Suffolk." "Why, boy?"

"They wanted to know if they followed the path up the hill, where they'd come out. I told them they'd come out on top."

Ephraim cast a withering glance at the hikers and said: — "Where the hell did they think they'd come out then? Ignorant bloody Londoners, I don't doubt."

A retired doctor over at Woodbridge told me that when one of his very old patients died, he attended the funeral. At the conclusion of the graveside service he overheard two old locals discussing the passing of their companion.

"How old were old Charl?"

"Eighty-five."

"How old be you, then?"

"Eighty-eight."

Pause for thought. And then:—

"Hardly worth your while goin' home."

* * *

A great day in Pin Mill would be the launching of a new smack. There was a boat shed half way up the lane, next to the *Riga Inn*. There thirty foot sailing smacks were built for fishing and stone dredging. Let me describe a launching day just as dear old Mrs Higgins told it to me.

"The half finished smack was wedged up on a 'rolley' and a pair of Suffolk punches loaned by the farmer across the way were shackled on and hove the boat up the steep slope out of the Riga dip and up into the lane. Then two check ropes were made fast each side of the rolley and we village schoolchildren held on to them to check the rolley down the hill to the hard, where the boat was duly decked and rigged before launching on the next spring tide. There was no school that day and we got a penny each for holding onto the ropes — boys one side and girls the other. It was a lovely day out for us."

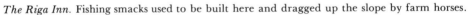

The Riga Inn. Fishing smacks used to be built here and dragged up the slope by farm horses.

CHAPTER EIGHT

Beaches which hold History

O N THE Felixstowe side of Harwich Harbour the foreshore is shingle, the pebbles rattling up and down as the tides ebb and flow or when they are beset by onshore winds. The seaward banks are dangerous to any sort of ship grinding on to them by some misfortune or careless navigation. On the Harwich side, which is in Essex, there is soft mud and rivers bounded by saltings and waving reeds. Suffolk seamen, bred among the greater dangers, often referred to Essex bargemen as "reed sparrows" because, it was averred, they rarely ventured far from their native shores and rivers. Even though the Essexmen often won the famous Thames and Medway barge races, Suffolk sailors didn't call that seafaring. "Regatta sailors" they would say, ploughing their lonely course to King's Lynn, the Humber ports and the Tyne. On a quiet night the rattle of shingle to a Suffolk ear helped guide him clear of danger.

The Suffolk shingle starts where Suffolk starts, on the Felixstowe beach; and continues east and north until we come to the sands of Norfolk in the Great Yarmouth area.

These pebbles hold a long history. They felt the tread of the early Christian missionary, St Felix, who came from Burgundy in Anglo-Saxon times, crowned one Sigebert as King of East Anglia in the seventh century, and left his own name to what is now known as a respectable modern holiday resort. The Felixstowe shingle also served as "bullets" against Dutchman de Ruyter's attempted invasion—the English firing their cannon balls into the beach in front of the invaders as told elsewhere in this volume.

A mile or two further east a bank of shingle bars the entrance to the River Deben, except to the knowledgeable mariners who know there is a way round the end of it. The port of Goseford used to flourish here, sending thirteen ships and some three hundred seamen to carry Edward the Third's soldiery to France and the Lowlands. I have never been able to trace the actual boundaries of this long forgotten Port of Goseford, but it seems to have covered the waters and shore side of what we now call Felixstowe Ferry. Perhaps it was originally nothing more than a ford for geese, large flocks of which used to be driven across country to the big towns and markets. They were generally driven by women. In this connection, although nothing to do with Suffolk, there is an ancient song taught to me by the late Jimmy Coles of Erith, a licensed London waterman of the old school. Some of Jimmy's verses about young lovers in the ferry-skiff cannot be printed here (or anywhere else!!) but I remember the verse about the Goose-girl: —

Then there came a young Goose girl from Stratford St Mary
And stood on the steps in a pretty despair
But she had not a ha'penny to pay for a wherry
And stood on the steps in a pretty despair
But she sang so sweet, she sang so merry
He put her and all of her geese in his wherry
And her pretty face was the fare for a ferry
And rowed her across to Farringdon Fair.

So perhaps the ancient Port of Goseford got its name from being the passage taken across the River Deben by the goose girls of Suffolk.

In its heyday Goseford was more important than Ipswich, and English kings looked with favour upon ships and men from the Deben. Suffolk seamen were reckoned among the best in the land, especially during the Plantagenet reigns. One Deben seaman's name has come down through the centuries because of his courage, toughness and endurance under terrifying hardships. He was John Fox of Woodbridge, and he was in a ship trading between Suffolk ports and the Eastern Mediterranean. About the year 1563 he and some of his crew were captured by "Turkish" pirates and made to work as galley slaves. For some fourteen years he slogged at the galley oars, half-starved and often lashed by the slave master's thong.

John Fox suffered and schemed until one day he saw the opportunity to make a desperate dash for freedom. Rallying his fellow slaves, he led them in a mutiny and rebellion at the Port of Alexandria. Robert Moore of Harwich was there too. They overpowered their guards, captured a galley and rowed to Crete, where they found shelter in a monastery. Many had died on the way. The monks informed the Pope of John Fox's escape and money was sent from Rome to despatch this valiant Christian seaman to the King of Spain, who had him serve as a master-gunner in his fleet for another two years. Eventually he was permitted to return to Woodbridge and was given a pension by our Queen Elizabeth. He later became Captain of his old ship, the *Mary Fortune*, and traded between Blythburgh and the Thames. He died in 1594 and left ten pounds "to the poor of Woodbridge".

Sailing along close to the shingle beaches of Suffolk in coastal sailing barges, I often thought of the worthy John Fox, working the same tides and much the same channels, listening to the music of the pebbles in a lazy onshore swell, and wondered if I, living some four hundred years later and with Suffolk blood in my veins, could ever be as bold as he. Thank heaven that my own misfortunes in a life at sea—on fire in the North Sea, sinkings and rescue in wartime, gales and distress—have never demanded the courage and endurance with which John Fox was blessed.

These pebbly beaches, desolate and bitterly cold in a Norseman's wind, could tell many a strange tale. The old Excisemen used to bury themselves in it up to the neck and thus hide in wait for smugglers to land their contraband boats. It was like this that they caught Margaret Catchpole, Will Laud and John Luff near Orfordness before they could escape to Flanders in the brig that was waiting for them in Hollesley Bay. Margaret Catchpole, a Levington girl who worked for the Cobbold family at Priory Farm near Ipswich, was wanted for horsestealing, Will Laud, her lover, for smuggling, and John Luff for murder.

Laud and Luff were shot dead on the shingle and Margaret Catchpole was eventually deported to Australia in 1801. She had previously been sentenced to death for stealing one of Mr Cobbold's horses from Priory Farm and riding seventy miles to Aldgate to join her lover. Horse stealing carried the death sentence in those days, but, through the good offices of her employer, Margaret's punishment was reduced to deportation. Laud was a native of Aldeburgh—shipwright and seaman.

Where John Luff originated no one seems to know, but he was an evil influence over Laud and his long knife had split the guts of more than one who dared to stand in his way. Suffolk was well rid of him. Some say his spirit still haunts the beach at Shingle Street, where the River Ore rushes out into Hollesley Bay at a rate of knots. His ghost is known by its piercing scream at night.

Suffolk barge discharging coal at Burnham-on-Crouch.

Shingle Street is no place for the unwary mariner. Great mounds of shingle rise up at spring tides when the wind is between east and south, only to disappear a few days later and emerge somewhere else.

"Them old knolls are rum things," the old pilot used to say. "We had a yacht near wrecked on one—tried to get in with no pilot. Had to employ labour to get him off—cost a pound. Pilotage is seven and six—comes out cheaper."

I remember when I was mate with Percy Quantrill in a barge many years ago we hove-to off Shingle Street to take the pilot aboard. We were bound to Snape maltings with a cargo of barley from London, before it was put out of use "and made into some sort of music-hall—more's the pity", to quote the comments of local people who had worked there for generations and hoped to work there again should it reopen. We used to take the barley right up the Ore and Alde, past Iken, to Snape Bridge. There was a pub there, the *Plough and Sail*, and still is, though nowadays tarted up for the "music-hall customers".

When I traded to Snape there was only one worker who had ever been to London and few had any idea what the term "music hall" meant. To them any hall where music was played was a music hall; for this quotation I must

Snape Maltings, where sailing barges used to unload barley and later in the year, load malt for the London breweries. Nowadays it is a music centre for the Aldeburgh Festival. No barley—no malt and mostly empty.

apologise to the charming Miss Imogen Holst and her fellow organisers who have worked so devotedly to establish the now famous Aldeburgh Festival of Music. Miss Holst once came to the *Plough and Sail* when we were having a song and dance session and joined in the fun with delightful enthusiasm and even tried to learn a step dance to my old melodeon. In fact she was half

The Plough and Sail, outside the Maltings where bargemen and maltsters used to refresh themselves. The old cabin-like bar used to resound with many a merry song and rural music, but not now.

inclined to get some of those old folk songs, and the singers, in the Festival, but I do not think the idea was ever adopted. One well known country character, Cyril Poacher of Blaxhall, walked all the way to Aldeburgh with the notion, sadly mistaken, that he would be asked to sing. But he could not understand "What was goin' on" and after a few pints walked home again.

Outside the pub back door was a well-worn stone bollard which had been used for centuries to moor the barley barges. It was the mate's duty to get ashore with a strong wire to go over the bollard to prevent the barge "slipping off" the mud on the ebb tide, away from the quay. This bollard, being right by the back door of the pub, was a good excuse for a quick pint while the skipper passed the other end round his windlass to heave tight. I remember the mate of the *Dorothy* singing out "all fast, skipper" and disappearing for two hours!

When the Shingle Street pilot came off to us in Hollesley Bay in his smart little white rowing boat, he welcomed us as though we had come from the other side of the world. "Good morning, Captain; good morning, Mr Mate. I hope you have had a good voyage. If you will kindly slack my boat astern we will shape for shore, with that first whelm on our port bow." (Whelm is a patch of disturbed water caused by an underwater shoal). He had an old-world courtesy, so lacking in modern times.

Then came an interesting exchange between my skipper and the pilot.

"How much water are you drawing, Captain?"

"Six foot. How much water over the bar?"

"Four foot. She'll just do it."

We "just did it"—riding over the shingle with a rumble and rattle as though we were on rollers. The barge soo'ed a foot out of the water, scoured on with the rushing tide, and into the deep water of the river. The old pilot dropped smartly into his boat and soon disappeared among the inshore desolation of the Shingle Street knolls towards his cottage.

To a seaman it is quite uncanny to go sweeping up the river behind the narrow shingle bank "on the wrong side" of Orfordness Lighthouse. The Keep of Orfordness Castle glowers down on you as you pass, it cost fourteen hundred

Orford Castle.

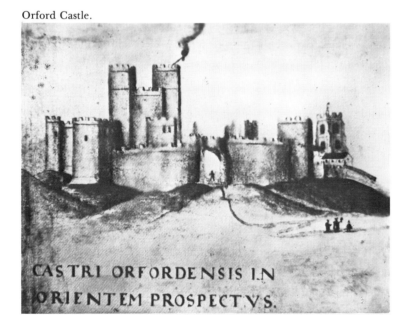

pounds to build in 1165, and you can almost feel the Norman guards watching from the battlements, ready to put an arrow through the skipper's neck if he gave them any reason to doubt his intentions. Even a hundred years after the Battle of Hastings, where the Norman victory was at the cost of terrible losses, they were still half afraid of the Angles and Saxons outside their fortress castles.

A strange creature came ashore on the shingle in Henry the Second's time, a naked man-like form covered with long hair and a long beard. It was written down by Ralph of Coggeshall that he "came up out of the sea", and was taken to Orford Castle, where Bartholomew de Gladville, the custodian, kept him prisoner, fed him, and tried to make him speak. But the wild creature kept silent, and ate meat ravenously, but first squeezing the blood out from it between his strong hands. He was even cruelly tortured to try and force some sound or word out of him.

One day his captors took him to the shore and allowed him to go into the sea at a place they had surrounded with nets: but he dived under them and escaped into deeper water, eventually coming back on shore again of his own accord. Once more he was taken to the Castle but a few days later he fled at great speed to the sea and was never seen again.

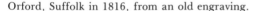

Orford, Suffolk in 1816, from an old engraving.

The story of this strange creature was so well recorded and witnessed that there can be little doubt that it is true. Some writers aver that he must have been a seal which has a head, eyes and whiskers rather like a "Colonel Blimp". But the shoreside population, especially those of Viking stock, were quite familiar with seals and had at times hunted them, so they were not likely to have one come ashore and think it was a man. Moreover his torturers at the Castle had once hung him up "by his feet" to try and make him talk.

To my knowledge this mystery has never been solved; but it is typical of the Suffolk manner of spanning the centuries that Percy Quantrill casually remarked; "They caught a wild man out of the sea here", as though it was

The author's first ship when a boy of fifteen.

St Bartholomew's Church, Orford, Suffolk.

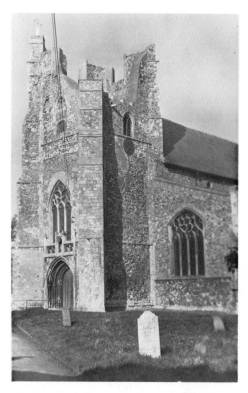

quite recent and not some nine hundred years ago. He had never read about it. He had heard his grandfather mention it.

The shingle beach can play some tricks on strangers. When I was Master of a steel barge named the *Greenhithe*, carrying cement and wheat to Yarmouth and Norwich, a small collier ran ashore between Orfordness and Aldeburgh and became a total wreck. A contractor cut her up for scrap and each day a lorry or two would come out from Aldeburgh for a load. Drivers were warned not to leave their lorries on the beach overnight, but one man, his vehicle half loaded, found he could not make the wheels grip. As it was getting dark he decided to leave it there until the morning, when he could find some help.

There was a moderate onshore breeze from the south east that night so when he came back in the morning the wheels had disappeared completely into the pebbles thrown up above the normal high water mark. No amount of effort with shovels and towing wires could free it and finally the lorry was abandoned. From aboard the barge we used to observe it each trip, slowly being engulfed by the shingle. The last we saw of it (three months later) was just the top of the driver's cab. Now it has completely disappeared from view,

An old "boomie" barge, name unknown, in the River Deben.

Suffolk crew on a Suffolk yacht at the turn of the century.

no doubt helping to build up the narrow shingle bank that protects Slaughden from the North Sea. Want a lorry?

Aldeburgh was a Danish settlement in ancient times. The famous English composer, the late Sir Benjamin Britten, lived there although he was actually born at Lowestoft on St Cecilia's Day (22nd November 1913). St Cecilia was the patron saint of music. Britten used to stroll the shingle beaches and listen intently to all the sounds he could hear there. These sounds, the cry of the gull, the rattle of pebbles, the tidal wash and the wind and waves, he noted down and in due course converted them to music. Each noise was to him a note of music and he only needed to arrange them in proper order to make them into his "Sea Interludes". They are called: — Dawn, Sunday Morning, Moonlight, Storm.

They were played during his opera about Peter Grimes, a Suffolk fisherman. Listen to these pieces and you could well be on Aldeburgh beach, where the old timbered Moot Hall stands. This ancient building is threatened with destruction by every onshore gale. Once the hall was the centre of the town but now it is a lonely monument to seaward of the more modern streets: although it is hardly correct to call anything in Aldeburgh modern. The only modern building I remember is the big *East Suffolk Hotel* where I and my crew were taken after our barge *Martinet* had been sunk by bombs off Orfordness in the Second World War. The Aldeburgh lifeboat came to our rescue as the old ketch went down at the crack of dawn. The coxswain could not beach his boat properly because of an anti-invasion boom, and as she hit, broadside on, we were shot out into the surf and dragged ashore by some Canadian soldiers. Local helpers soon had us in the *East Suffolk Hotel* and I have a hazy memory of sitting in a hot bath and being plied with glasses of hot whisky. This, on top of the rum we had been given in the lifeboat, produced in us a sort of "don't care" attitude and made our losses and hardships seem much lighter. A dear old lady representing the Aldeburgh branch of the Shipwrecked Mariners Association then went round the town clainging a huge bell and shouting; "Bring out your clothes for the shipwrecked mariners". And, bless them, they did; clothing us in all sorts of strange garbs and setting us off to our homes with warm handshakes and "Good Luck" messages in broad Suffolk.

One who professed to hate the Suffolk people, and those at Aldeburgh in particular, was the poet George Crabbe. Judging by his biting and vicious sentiments his name ought to have been spelt "Crabby"—for he certainly seems to have been a disagreeable old crab. He wrote that Suffolk people were: —

> A wild amphibious race with sullen woe displayed in every face
> Who far from civil arts and social fly and scowl at strangers with
> suspicious eye.

The Moot Hall on Aldeburgh beach; the eroding North Sea has pushed the town inland to firmer ground.

Perhaps the local inhabitants scowled at him with some justification because he started life aboard a fishing boat, could not do well at that, so became a shipwright at Aldeburgh. He didn't do much good at that either, so he tried his hand as an apothecary in the town. The Aldeburgh people, knowing him as a job-hopping jack of all trades and master of none, did not put much faith in his administrations, so he cleared out of his native county for nearly thirty years and wrote poetry under the benign patronage of the wealthy Duke of Rutland. And, blow me, if he doesn't turn up in Aldeburgh again as curate of the local church, but he still had that jaundiced view of the coastal population whom he called:

A bold, artful, surly, savage race.

I was told that "people round here didn't go a lot on him. Crab by name and crab by nature". This was the comment of an old retired person at nearby Walberswick.

The late King George the Sixth used to love this bit of coastline. He did a bit of shooting in nearby Benacre Woods and later started a boys camp near Southwold. And I believe he used to come down from London to see the lads and share their meals on all sorts of informal occasions. I saw him once, and I have never seen anyone look more like a king — a handsome countenance, blue eyes and wavy golden hair. And I know he had the courage of a lion. If the Germans had invaded this country he was prepared to fight it out to the last. Retreat to Canada or the United States? Not him! He was practising every day with automatic firearms in the grounds of Buckingham Palace. He might have become another King Alfred, with Germans instead of Danes to beat back.

CHAPTER NINE

Men of Kessingland

WHERE the Suffolk shingle ends and the Norfolk sands begin and the River Waveney divides the "north folk" from the "south folk", the village of Kessingland teeters on the edge of a low cliff, its base for long undermined by the wash of the pebbles. My mother Anne Sarah Brown, was born there, and her many uncles and cousins; but that row of cottages facing the sea tumbled down onto the beach long, long ago. The bricks and chimney pots can still be seen half-buried on the beach. For generations they braved the east wind, until their foundations were cut from under them. The occupants retreated slowly inland, to Pakefield, Kirkley and Lowestoft, leaving little Kessingland to the ravages of speculators who specialised in holiday chalets and caravans and all that goes with such features. They now spread across the higher slopes like some white spotted disease, cheek by jowl, closer than the pleasure seekers live in the cities of their daily labours. But there are still a few native long-liners working in open boats off the beach and they are some of the few left in England who employ this very expert method of fishing.

Kessingland High Street as it is today. Note Dave Kennard with Jacob.

Old cottages at Kessingland.

Records suggest that an old Viking family, the Kessings, settled here and gave name to the place. If this be true they were on the wrong side of the Waveney, which is the boundary between Norfolk and Suffolk. It has always been presumed that the "north folk" were predominantly of Norse descent and the "south folk" were the Anglian followers of the great Uffa and his tribe, who turned south after they had pulled their ships up the estuary of the Yare. There are certainly two distinct dialects, Norfolk being harsher and more guttural than the soft sing-song of Suffolk.

Kessingland's thatched church of St Edmund is not as big as its mighty tower suggests and the tombstones round it mark the last resting places of the Browns, Uttings and Kings; all related as far as I have been able to trace, and nearly all seamen and fishermen. The front of the pulpit is a ship's wheel, so that the person can grasp the spokes to give emphasis to his sermons.

My grandfather, Charles Brown, forged a strange link between Kessingland and a great hall in London. I hope the reader will be patient enough to let me relate the story.

He was a sick man at a rather early age and had to give up fishing with his brothers in the heavy old smacks they owned and worked on the Dogger Bank. But he was a good carpenter and shipwright and specialised in artistic scroll work carved and picked out in gold leaf on the bow and stern of every one of their six vessels. He was thus engaged one day in Lowestoft and was being

watched by a Scotsman named Aird, whose firm was building the quay of what
is now Lowestoft Harbour. When Grandfather climbed up off the staging
which he had slung across the smack's counter, Mr Aird said: —

"I have been admiring your handiwork and I would like to take you to my
house at Warnham in Sussex to carve the oak beams."

It was a huge mansion house with scores of great oak beams, and
Grandfather, a very sick man by then and unable to work long hours in the cold
winds of Lowestoft, was glad to accept the job and was given a cottage in the
grounds. It took him two years to complete this work, and then he feared he
might be dismissed.

"Now I've got another job for you," he was told, "we are building a great
hall in London and we want all the beam ends carved as you have done these."
The worthy Charlie Brown was duly conveyed to London and his work can be
seen there today. The building is called the Royal Albert Hall.

Nearly a hundred years later I was asked to sing there at the English Folk
Festival. My youngest daughter also joined me in an old East Anglian fishing
song, "Still I love him, I'll forgive him": and thus the rather quaint family

St Edmund's Church, Kessingland. The roof is thatched and many of the gravestones mark the
author's ancestors—Browns and Uttings.

Appropriately a ship's wheel
is a part of the pulpit in
St Edmund's Church,
Kessingland.

ANNE ROBERTS

connection with this famous building was kept alive. Previously, in the days of
the Great Depression of the 1920s, when I was an out-of-work sailorman,
picking up a few pounds as a prize fighter in Blackfriars Ring and Premierland,
I had fancifully pictured myself fighting at the Albert Hall on the same bill as
such famous men as Georges Carpentier, Joe Beckett and Bombadier Billy
Wells. Fortunately for me I never reached such eminence and found a ship
instead. But I was glad to sing there.

My grand-uncle Louis Brown was perhaps the most famous of my
mother's Kessingland family. Tired of fishing, he sailed away in a three

masted barque and did not get home again for seven years. This may have been his own fault, for on one occasion in San Francisco he jumped ship and was up a tree watching her sail out of the Golden Gate with her flag at half mast for him. Later he sailed to the North West Passage in search of Franklin and was frozen up there for two years. His ship was named the *Diane*. It was in 1845 that Franklin set out with two ships, the *Erebus* and the *Terror* to find a North West Passage, but the ships became icebound. Relief expeditions were sent but neither Franklin nor any of his men were ever found.

A seaman's last berth—one of the Utting family in Kessingland churchyard.

The Norman Gateway, Bury St Edmunds.

Figure of St Edmund over an office in Bury St Edmunds.

Said to be the smallest pub in England, *The Nutshell*, Bury St Edmunds.

Barge Race Day.

A few years ago, walking round the exhibition on board the *Cutty Sark* at Greenwich, Mr Frank Carr, the Maritime Museum Director at that time, pointed out to me the figurehead of a ship named the *Diane*, which, he said, had once gone in search of Franklin in the North West Passage. This figurehead had been dug up in a garden in Kent. I know now that grand-uncle Louis had lain off Greenhithe (Kent) in London River for something like three months and stayed in an old pub named the *White Hart*. Many is the pint I drank in there when I sailed in Everard's coasting barges before an old aunt told me, "That's where your Uncle Louis stayed when he was in the *Diane*."

One of the Brown family's sailing drifters. Note registration letters L.T. but, to quote a local saying, "There are more Lowestoft smacks owned in Kessingland than in Lowestoft."

The old pleasure steamer on the Orwell.

From H. W. Moffat's collection

When he was away for seven years his wife only had letters from him at the rate of about one a year, brief and never very newsy. He was a stoical man of few words, and when one day his wife was working in the house thinking that he was probably some thousands of miles away she was startled to see him strolling past the kitchen window. She flew to the back door, flung it open, and there he stood regarding her. After his seven years' absence she was dumbfounded and speechless. But he wasn't. Stroking his long yellow beard he said: — "Coo — don't you look old!"

When the cottage tumbled into the sea he shifted to Beccles and died there, but the church authorities have smothered his grave and I cannot find it. He had paid for it, too!

CHAPTER TEN

People who made Suffolk

$\mathbf{F}$ROM the northernmost limit of Suffolk's shingle beaches, the quickest way to get to my cottage at Pin Mill was by sea, especially with a wind out of the north west. But it would be doing Suffolk an injustice if I did not venture inland, along the banks of the Waveney and south about, much the same as Wuffa and his tribesmen of the old Anglian race.

The *Anglo-Saxon Chronicle* of 449 A.D. records that the British chief Vortigern "invited the Angles hither . . . then they fought against the Picts and had victory wherever they came. Then they sent to Angel (their home on the Continent) to send more aid and to be told of the worthlessness of the Britons and the excellence of the land . . . from Angel, which has stood waste ever since . . . came the East Angles, Middle Angles, Mercians and all the Northumbrians."

They were descended from Woden, "and from this Woden sprang all our Royal Family and that of the peoples dwelling south of the Humber". King Alfred was descended from Woden, and, according to some genealogists, so are our Royal Family of today.

The East Anglians came from Schleswig, on the Danish-German border, which district was completely deserted and left derelict, the whole nation, men, women and children, having crossed the North Sea to Britain. Danish archaeologists excavated the old Anglian homeland some years ago and found evidence and remnants of a farming community which had apparently ceased on migration to a Britain left defenceless by the Romans. The land of Angel has been disputed by Denmark and Germany ever since. The more warlike Saxons dwelt to the south of them, and the Jutes to the north, but all spoke dialects of English and were probably branches of the original tribe from southern Sweden. To think of these tall, fair haired people (not unlike the Scandinavians of today) climbing up the low cliffs from the ships grounded on the shingle and tramping inland to Beccles, Bungay, Hoxne and all the neat little villages of West Suffolk; rowing up the rivers to Blythburgh, Woodbridge and Ipswich, gives us a picture of the kingdom of East Anglia being created. The Celtic British tribes, brave but out-numbered, fought and were slaughtered, captured as slaves, or driven westward. For centuries there was little or no Celtic element in East Anglia, though perhaps some continued to exist in the Iceni region of the River Waveney and in south Suffolk. The

English found them swift runners and excellent horsemen, and used a few of them as mercenaries and messengers. I doubt if the invaders had ever seen horses and chariots used with such skill and dexterity, the British warriors running up and down the shafts and over the horses' backs to use their spears and javelins while dashing along at full speed. But they had been softened and subjugated by the Romans for too long to make any sort of organised stand against these sturdy fighting men from the north.

The town of Bungay retains a link with its Anglo-Saxon past. It still has a "Town Reeve", which every sizable town had in those days. The title "Mayor" is non-English and smacks of Norman rule. I have read that a small band of Englishmen took the town and named it after their family — Bonn. They called it Bun- inega-haye, which means the property of the Bonn tribe.

In later, Norman, times the notorious Bigods took it over. When Sir Hugh Bigod had one of his many quarrels with King Henry the Second, he shouted from the walls of Framlingham Castle: —

> Were I in my castle of Bungay
> I would ne care for the king of Cockney

But he found that the East Anglians did not care a lot about him either, or any of his bigoted and tyrannical descendants. To try and oppress a Suffolker and really "get him down" was like using a sledge-hammer to try and flatten a sponge.

Bungay is the Black Shuck country. Some call him the Black Dog of Bungay, harbinger of terror and foreboding. On the old Corn Cross there used to be a panel inscribed: —

> All down the church in midst of fire
> The hellish monster flew
> And passing onwards to the Quire
> He many people slew.

This, I was told by a local publican, commemorated a wild and stormy night in 1577, when houses in Bungay were struck by lightning, people killed, and the town flooded. Black Shuck has got a lot to answer for in Suffolk but nearly all the stories about him seem to trace back to the warlike and rebellious Bigod family, who tried for generations to break the spirit of the native Anglians. And failed.

To walk the lanes of West Suffolk and see the well-cared-for farmland, it is as well to remember that it was originally cleared, drained and brought into cultivation by Wuffa and his followers some fourteen hundred years ago. They were land-seekers above all else, and the savagery of the advance guard, wary soldiers in a strange country, was not the nature of the Wuffingas. Neither the Britons nor the Romans had ever farmed the lowlands of Suffolk, but the

English had had many years experience on the low lying stretches of their native Angel. But they had "farmed it out" and were quick to devote their inbred husbandry to the fertile acres of Suffolk beyond the coastal strip. In fact nearly all the English were either sailors or farmers—the two skills which are still predominant in the Englishman of today. Give him a ship and he'll go a'roving. Give him some land and he will make two blades of grass grow where only one grew before.

The Bury St Edmunds area is full of English history although the town itself, having once been burned to the ground, is not now particularly impressive apart from the Abbey. St Edmund the King is said to have been buried there after the Danes shot him to death with arrows against an old oak tree. At Hoxne the remains of a great oak still stand in an open meadow and a number of arrow heads were found in it. But any broad oak served as a target for archers over the centuries and no one has yet proved (or even attempted to prove) that the arrow heads were of Danish origin. If they were they would be over a thousand years old.

The old Abbey ruins at Bury St Edmunds.

The Magna Carta Stone, to be
found in the old Abbey ruins.

Ruins. Bury St Edmunds.

At nearby Hoxne is Goldbrook Bridge under which, it is claimed, King Edmund was hiding after his defeat and flight from the invading Danes. There is a plaque on the Bridge to this effect, which impresses tourists but is disputed by those who think he was killed and buried at "Suthune" (Sutton). His body was no doubt taken to Bury St Edmunds which was originally called Bedericsworth: and his severed head later on, after some monks found it in a wood, being guarded by a huge wolf. Perhaps the ghost of that wolf became the terrible monster dog Black Shuck of later years!

In Ipswich one day I met a party of American Ladies on a pilgrimage to Bury St Edmunds. Of St Edmund they knew little but they called themselves "Women of the Magna Carta" — all descended, so they told me, from the Barons who, in 1214, swore to make King John sign the famous document. These charming ladies had with them a Press Agent to prove it. To their credit it must be said that there are thousands of Americans of Suffolk origin, though I doubt if they could trace their ancestry back as far as 1214.

American airmen made Suffolk an important base in the Second World War and in many an old pub you can find photographs and letters from those amiable allies who fitted so easily into Suffolk life, and apparently enjoy happy memories of their service here. One of them laughingly told me in a train: —

"If you ask an Englishman the way in one of these funny old towns, he'll say 'Go down this road until you see a little alleyway leading to the *Crown and Anchor*, cross the road to the Church and cut through the litten to the *Shipwrights' Arms*, turn left at the War Memorial, over a little footbridge, turn right by the *Kings' Arms*' — and he'll always finish up with 'and you can't miss it'."

I was at Lavenham one day when there were some American tourists strolling round the ancient streets, looking at one of the best examples in existence of a fifteenth century town, when I noticed down Water Street some old weavers' cottages which were built before America had been discovered, and are still lived in.

There was a famous family named de Vere centuries ago in Lavenham. Records say they came over with William the Conqueror, but there is evidence that they were landlords here before then. One of them was named Albericke, which does not sound like Norman-French, but rather Flemish. One of the de Veres fought with distinction in the Crusades and the name still lingers on in Lavenham.

This book was printed in Lavenham and if a copy or two still exists in a hundred years time, in Suffolk, America, Australia, or any part of the world, I shall count it as my very, very tiny contribution to the timelessness of Suffolk.

Wool towns and villages in West Suffolk are all quaint and pleasant to visit. Some of them have been untouched and unspoilt for hundreds of years. In the pubs you find square, solid, honest looking men who make you feel you could trust them on first sight. They are friendly to strangers, too, in their quiet way, but you need to be quiet yourself as they will soon turn away from a loud mouth. Very different from East Suffolk where a loud mouth is quickly shut up with what the Cockneys call a "bunch of fives".

The Woolpit village sign featuring the "green children", church and wolf.

The whole of western Suffolk, the open country, the well husbanded farmland, the quaint "picturebook" villages and well ordered little towns and the steady reliable people, breathes an atmosphere of serene tranquillity. Let no man disturb it. It is a precious piece of old England — Long Melford, Brent Eleigh, Monks Eleigh, Kersey, Nayland, Bergholt, Framlingham, Hengrave, Woolpit, Clare, Hadleigh — everyone worth a roll of film and a sketch book and a whole day of unhurried exploration, as well as a browse into local history.

Woolpit holds a secret which may never be solved — part history, part legend and part folklore. It concerns the story of the Babes in the Wood, well known in Norfolk and Suffolk. There is factual evidence that in the Middle Ages a Norfolk earl wished to dispose of two small children who were the rightful owners of large estates. He was their guardian, probably their uncle, and had a claim on these rich lands if the two little ones failed to grow to maturity. So he told two of his henchmen to murder them; but one of them could not bring himself to commit such a deed and persuaded his companion that they should be taken into the great forest (Thetford?) and abandoned there, so at least no cruel blow would be struck. This was done.

The wicked earl had at first tried to poison the children by daily putting small quantities of arsenic in their food, their little bodies growing weaker and weaker. One of the henchmen knew of this and thought they would die in the forest in any case without the necessity of brutal murder to torment his conscience for the rest of his life.

So the children were left under a tree in the dark forest, fell asleep, and woke to find that it was only twilight when the sun should have been up. The forest growth was too dense and they thought they were in some land of perpetual twilight. But they survived, possibly on nuts and berries, and wandered hand in hand until they came to an old wolfpit. This wolfpit was outside a small village and they walked along the bottom of it until they heard voices and saw the light of the sun.

Woolverstone Church.

Old church porch, Woolverstone.

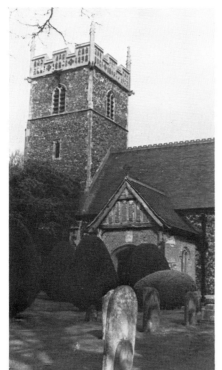

Now hear the Woolpit version of the story. Some farmhands working in a field near the village were astonished to see two little children "come up out of the ground" — and they had green faces. Fearing that they were hobgoblins of some sort the labourers at first ran away but later brought some local people back, who took the babes to the village and cared for them.

The green children coming up out of the wolf pit at Woolpit. Were these the babes in the wood?

It is a fact that arsenic, taken in small doses over a long period, will give the skin a greenish hue and the story was carried down through the generations of Woolpit dwellers, that two green children had once "come up out of the ground". They were given a diet of meat and vegetables and gradually their green skin altered to a normal colour, but the boy was too sickly to survive and soon died. The little girl, however, recovered completely, grew up and married. I was told that there are still people in Woolpit who are "descended from the green children" but no one would tell me who they were.

A radio investigator once tried to find out who in Woolpit were descended from the green babes, but all he got was a wry smile, a shake of the head and a shrug. Either they didn't know, or wouldn't tell.

Thetford forest is still a dense but beautiful mass of trees where wildlife can exist undisturbed by motor traffic, noisy folk and picnic parties, who have to restrict themselves to places reserved for such visitors. Away from the tea flasks, sandwich papers, cars and coaches there are herds of deer. At the slightest crack of a twig underfoot they flash away through the trees so quickly that you cannot be sure whether you have seen them or not. It must have taken a good archer to bring one down in the old days! I should think he would have to lie in wait for hours and hours before he had the chance of a shot.

The town of Thetford, which is just across the border in Norfolk, was named after the little river Thet, used to be a regular battleground between English and Danes. In various places nearby are groups of mounds which mark the dead of both armies. There is a great earthen mound called Thetford Castle, but it does not look much like a castle now. I suppose the main fortifications stood on top of the mound, which itself may have been, originally, an Iron Age earth fort on the lines of Maiden Castle or Badbury Rings in Dorset. King Canute made Thetford his capital for a short time and died there some fifty years before the tragic Battle of Hastings. Canute's great friend and adviser, Earl Godwin, had a house there and became the premier English statesman in the reign of Edward the Confessor. It was the sons of Godwin and their followers from East Anglia and Wessex, who took on the might of Normandy (all too hastily) and died defending their country on a blood-soaked hill in Sussex. The northern earls let them down; failed to arrive with their armies; and retreated from London to the north when they heard that all the Godwins had been slain. Had they taken the field with King Harold there would never have been a Norman "Conquest". It was never a conquest: rather a take-over of a divided nation.

The deep history of all these West Suffolk towns and villages has interested many researchers and writers, so I will go back to Pin Mill, where I started this book. But first I would have to travel into East Suffolk via Stowmarket and Ipswich. The only distinction of the Stowmarket district is that it sheltered what seems to have been generations of traitors and assassins, the Tyrells. It was Sir Walter Tyrell who was blamed for sending a well-aimed arrow into the heart of William the "Conqueror's" successor, William Rufus, Rufus the Red, while hunting in the New Forest. There is a stone in the forest to mark the spot.

Rufus may not have been as bad a king as historians make out and the East Anglians and West Saxons gladly fought under him at the second Battle of Hastings when Robert of Normandy and his earls landed at Pevensey, just as the old Duke had done, to throw Rufus off the throne. Imagine the joyful revenge of the Anglo-Saxons when they drove the Norman knights into the sea. It helped to wipe out the grief of King Harold's defeat, even though they were led by a Norman king and no doubt had some assistance from Normans resident in England. Another Stowmarket Tyrell by the name of James is said to have admitted that he murdered the little Princes in the Tower in the reign of Richard the Third; but Henry the Seventh had Tyrell's head lopped off after the Battle of Bosworth Field.

Stowmarket is connected to Ipswich by the River Gipping and in 1789 a canal was dug, utilising much of the river. Trade was booming and the idea was to get ships up inland from the Orwell. It was too shallow to be a success and the Ipswich authorities, not wishing to divert cargoes from their own quays, were not exactly helpful. It is silted up and grown over now, but still visible. Once a Pin Mill fisherman, unable to get a decent price for his catch in Ipswich, sailed his smack up the canal to Stowmarket and sold the fish for a better figure there. I doubt if his loss of time made it worthwhile, but at least he was able to cock a snook at the tight-fisted Ipswich dealers.

There's not much local fish brought to Ipswich nowadays. I used to take a good catch of sole to a certain firm in the town when I was trawling with the *Stormy Petrel* — IH 57. They would only pay me 1/6d (7½p) a pound and on my way back to Pin Mill I saw they had them in the window at 3/6d (17½p) a pound. This firm boasted that they always supported "the local man". Their prices didn't support me, and I went back to a barge for a living.

There used to be a crazy fisherman on the Orwell by the name of Thomas Colson. He lived some hundred years ago and his only home was a leaky old smack, with patched, rotting sails. Today he might be called a religious fanatic. All about him were hung charms and texts, and he was apparently under the impression that a horde of devils were after him. He had old bones, tin pans, rings, a skull and various spells to keep them off. Many of the things tied to his arms and legs and body were articles which had come up from the river-bed in his trawl. Locally he was nicknamed "Robinson Crusoe" and several old people at Pin Mill had "heard tell of him". His tall, spare figure, aquiline features and piercing eyes made him an unforgettable figure.

His boat eventually sank in a severe north-west gale, and poor Thomas went with it, refusing all offers of help because he was sure the storm was the work of the devils tormenting him and that his numerous charms would frustrate their evil intentions. If his charms could have stopped the tide from rising, he and his boat might have been saved. But Suffolk tides have always broken loose in the north-west gales, springs or neaps, and nothing will stop them.

Pin Mill has been flooded more times than anyone can remember and old cottage walls show the marks and ravages of many a salt-water invasion. One day a big tide flowed into the cottage gardens and the inhabitants were busy "pugging up", which meant digging up wet clay from near the house and using it to caulk doors and any other openings. Properly done, and in good time, it was far more effective than the sandbagging used in modern times by immigrants from the cities. The pug was pressed into all possible openings and a retaining board nailed across the door posts to hold it in position. While all this was going on, one man sat in his cottage grieving over the death of his old father. The coffin had been made by a local shipwright and rested with its occupant on the front room table. Suddenly realising that the tide was coming up the garden path, the bereaved one thought about the safety of his pig and promptly splashed down to the sty and brought it into the shelter of the cottage. The water rose higher and higher, over the floorboards, until the pig was up to its belly. Pigs are very vulnerable to shock; and this was how the story was told to me: —

"I set there with me seaboots on and there's the old chap in his coffin on the table. Then I looks at the pig and the tide's still a'comin' and I reckon he's goin' to drown. We only had a small table so there's nothin' for it but take the old man off and put the pig on the table. As you know, Bob, old Harry was as good a boat builder as you'd find anywhere this side of Fiddler's Green, and that coffin he made for the old chap was as tight as a bottle. There was the old pig, happy as a lark, sittin' up on the table with a bowl of swill and the old man, he's a swirlin' round and round as the tide come in the door — never made a drop of water. When the ebb come away he lay there dry as a bone. The old chap had nothing to lose but that pig was worth a tidy few quid so I reckon I done right."

I have not permission to mention the name of the pig owner, but every one in Pin Mill knew the story of the well-caulked coffin.

Probably the oldest business still working in Pin Mill is under the name of Webb. The family originated in Littlehampton but were established as "Wheelwrights and Shipwrights" at Pin Mill in 1830. They have an old document to prove it. Their work probably alternated between farm carts, barges and fishing-boats. Nowadays they are boat builders and repairers and run a small chandlery for yachtsmen.

The late Ted Webb was one of the best barge-wrights I have ever seen at work. Without the aid of any mechanical equipment he could fit a heavy oak plank in the round of a barge's bow by knocking out the "trunnels" (tree-nails — wooden pegs used to fasten a barge's planks) and using the holes to fix long staves to the part under repair. Then the plank would be heated up on the common by a bonfire raging round an old pipe filled with water. When the plank had been there long enough according to Ted's judgement, he would come round the cottages and request help to run it down the Hard to the barge. We would all turn out with rags and sacks to protect us from scalding and trot down to the waiting Ted, who was inside the barge ready to draw the plank into position. The staves were then hauled tight with tackles across the barge — a few temporary bolts and the job was as good as done. Few, if any, would know how to set about that sort of work nowadays. Ted's final words were always: —

"Thank you gentlemen. The beer's in the *Butt*" — that was by way of appreciation for assistance rendered.

Ted Webb was a craftsman of a very ancient school and many of the expressions he used in the course of his work are quite unknown today, "snottle-dogs", "griper", "boll", "joggle" and a score of others which mystified local boating people. He put a "snottle-dog" in the stern of my barge *Cambria* one night when she broke out leaking with a cargo of wheat in her. I sailed her on to a mud flat and Ted and his sons trudged out to her at low water with only a Tilley lamp to work by. A knot in a plank had become loose so Ted drew it out and made a wooden plug the exact shape of the knot. The plug was coated with a mixture of pitch and tar and a layer of horse hair stuck round it while it was tacky. This was driven into the knot-hole with great force, cut off flush with the planking, and a tingle nailed over the outer end. That was in 1954 and it is there to this day, tight as ever.

"She's all right now," Ted told me when he had finished and came down the cabin for a mug of tea. "I've just put a snottle-dog in her. She won't leak no more."

Jack Powell, the Pin Mill sailmaker, whose mother was a distant relative of my father's family, was another fine old craftsman. He and Ted Webb had a curious liaison over the years. If Jack's roof leaked or some woodwork wanted repairing in the cottage, he would call Ted over to mend it. But Jack never paid him. If Ted wanted a canvas cover made, he would call Jack over to measure and make it. But Ted never paid him. Each told me at various times of the work he had done for the other "and he's never paid me a penny for it". But neither demanded payment! And by the time they were both close to departing this life it "wasn't worth bothering about".

One day a well known yachtswoman, who went in for "ocean racing" in the days of straight stems and long keels, came striding into Jack's loft with an urgent order.

"Jack, we'd have won that race if we'd had a decent reaching foresail. Can you make me a new one for the last race in a fortnight's time?"

Never one to be rushed, Jack looked a bit askance. "I doubt if I've got the canvas for that. And it takes a fortnight to get it sent here."

"Well, do your best," she said, "and if you can't get it done in time we'll have it for the first race next season."

The lady did not get her reaching foresail for the last race and in fact I suspect the worthy Jack had not even got round to ordering the canvas. The yacht was duly laid up for the winter at Pin Mill and near Christmastime the owner came down to see that all was well and buy a few drinks for the locals in the *Butt*. She then strode into Jack's sail loft.

"Where's my new reaching foresail, Jack? Let's have a look at it."

Jack put on an expression of complete surprise:— "Reaching foresail? This is Christmas, snowin' and blowin'. This ain't the weather for reaching foresails."

"Well, get it done as soon as you can."

Three months later the good lady called on Jack again. No reaching foresail. A month later, the sailing season very near and still no reaching foresail. By this time her patience was almost exhausted, much as she liked the dear old sailmaker.

"Look here Jack; you've had this order since last August and now it's April and the first race is next Saturday. I want that reaching foresail aboard **next Saturday morning**."

Jack nodded. "Saturday morning. Right. You shall have it."

On the Friday night the yacht's crew came trooping down the lane to prepare for an early muster the following day. The lady owner made straight for the sail loft and confronted the worthy Jack who was sitting on his low wooden bench quietly winding a ball of twine, slowly and carefully, as though he had not a care in the whole wide world. There was no sign of any new sail lying about.

"Now," says she, "where's my reaching foresail?"

Jack looked up, his bright blue eyes wide with astonishment.

"You said Saturday. This is Friday."

For a few moments the lady was speechless with anger and frustration. Then she stamped her foot, spun on her heel, and let out a single vehement comment:— "Bloody Suffolk", and stalked out.

That night the lamp in Jack's sail loft was seen to be still alight when the *Butt and Oyster* shut at half past ten.

Aboard the yacht next morning the crew were about early and the lady owner was curious to see a new sail bag on the foredeck. She told the crew to open it and they drew out a brand new, beautifully made, hand-stitched reaching foresail. There was a moment's silence. Then she burst out laughing until the tears rolled down her cheeks.

"Bloody Suffolk, they never change — thank God."

CHAPTER ELEVEN

The Village Changes

THERE is a new Pin Mill now; a Pin Mill which caters for the car and the holiday maker, the weekender and "way-out" characters unknown only a few years ago. No longer does rotund Jack Powell sit on his bench making sails under the old oak beams. His "loft", which had a permanent aroma of tar, hemp and canvas is a yacht shop now, where the needs of amateur sailors are catered for.

No longer does Ted Webb hammer out chain plates and leeboard toggles for barges in his tiny smithy in the "Pit". There are suburban type bungalows there now and the hillside looks more like the outcrop of an industrial town than the slope where we used to shoot and snare rabbits, and the occasional longtail. No longer does Harry King build the best boats on the east coast (or so we always reckoned). It's a car park now and there's another behind the old Maltings from which the smell of plastics emerges. No longer do bargemen and fishermen live in the cottages across the common. They have been altered and tarted up to suit retired folk and the tastes of the weekenders. Even our splendid old village patriarch and "Mayor", Ephraim Sharman, has to live in a council house in the next village. Harbour Master George Burroughes has passed away and I hope he is rewarded in Heaven for all the laughs he has given us with his stories and dry humour over pints in the *Butt*. Bill Simpson an old ex-barge hand, who once served in the flyer barge *Imperial*, occupied his part of Lark Cottages until his death, darkened though his windows were by the extensions of the cottage next door. Bill was the oldest surviving native of Pin Mill and lived all his life in the cottage where he was born.

At one time, every cottage across the common — Rose Cottages, Lark Cottages, Dwiny Cottage, Orwell Cottage, River View, Grindle Cottage and Albert Cottages — was occupied by bargemen and fishermen. They sailed, fished, hunted with their cunning old lurcher dogs, drank vast quantities of beer, and lived a life which has gone for ever. Perhaps the last taste of tradition in the hamlet was when Jill Roberts walked the Common path in her bridal gown to wed an Essex Morris Dancer in 1970. To the dancing of the Colchester Morris Men and the merry music of melodeons and concertinas and fiddles outside the church and the *Butt and Oyster*, the pair were sent off to uproarious cheers and the firing of the Mayor's 12-bore shotgun.

The ancient *Butt and Oyster Inn* looks out over modern Pin Mill.

Coal being unloaded on Pin Mill Hard from the barge *Our Boys.*
Photograph by courtesy of H. W. Moffat

But, turn your back on the hamlet and look out across the River Orwell and it is as beautiful as ever. The landlord of the *Butt and Oyster*, Pat Watts, has, to his everlasting credit, resisted such things as juke boxes, one-armed bandits, pintables and the like and kept the old inn as it should be—the ancient and unchanging centre of Pin Mill.

One example of the changing face of the little hamlet is the building now used as a yachtsmen's club. This was a wooden shed erected by old Squire Berners of Woolverstone Hall for Fred King, a local boat builder. Fred used to build boats under an old canvas shelter at the back of Lark Cottage and the old squire, doing the rounds of his estate one day said: "Is that the only place you've got to build boats, Fred?" And he promptly ordered a stout wooden shed to be built on the rising ground and from there the worthy Fred launched some splendidly-built boats by slinging a tackle from the overhanging branch of a big tree. A man named Gus King succeeded him. Old Harry King, who put natural grown timbers in his boats, strongly disapproved of Gus King using timbers steamed to shape. "There he is, putting in steamed timbers and him a

East Suffolk Morris Dancers.

Methodist!" There were a lot of traditional old crafts in the boat building trade along the East Anglian and Essex coasts before the days of fibre glass. They were rigid in their methods and used a knowledge gained over many generations. Blue prints were anathema to most of them and Frank Shuttlewood at Paglesham had an overlying principle: — "If it looks wrong, it **is** wrong." He used to build one smack every winter, his only assistant being a half-wit lad from the village to hold the nails and fastenings. A thirty-two foot smack would cost £600. Years ago, he and his father built a hundred ton barge, on their own, in six weeks. He once said to me: — "Nowadays, it would take some of them six weeks to find out how to start."

The old bargemen's footpath along the shore from Ipswich Docks.

Chelmondiston Church tower used to be a navigational mark for incoming ships.

Ted Webb, the last bargewright in Pin Mill, who died in 1963 after the last professional barge match, succeeded Gus King in Squire Berners' old shed. Soon, he was ousted to make room for the yachtsmen and the old boatshed resounded to pop tunes on a record player and the swish of young dancers on a polished floor. Something of a contrast to the old "Butt Ball", with sailing ship crews, of all nationalities, bargemen and villagers dancing on the green and playing skittles for copper kettles at the *Riga Inn* up the lane. There used to a fair at Pin Mill every Whitsuntide and the old people (now departed this life) have described to me how the lane was lined with stalls selling home-made cakes and sweets, and prunes at ten a penny; roundabouts on the hard ground of the Common, waterside frolics and a tug of war between the *Butt and Oyster* and the *Riga Inn*. There were wrestling matches and running races and even a women's mud race in the soft ooze at low water. People came from all over the surrounding villages and Mrs Higgins once counted seventy-two horses tethered on the common. And over at the gate of the Maltings always a tub of spiced beer and a big tin mug for the thirsty merry-makers. The Ruffles family owned the Maltings and also farmed land between Pin Mill and Shotley. All the sons went to sea in coasting barges and several were drowned in the winter storms. The last survivor was Bob Ruffles who died at the ripe old age of ninety-one and was barge-master for the Ipswich firm of R. & W. Paul. I knew him as a fine and fearless seaman who climbed the bar-post in the *Butt* on his eighty-fifth birthday. His Pin Mill has gone forever, but thousands of yachtsmen and holidaymakers have spent many happy days in and around this tiny hamlet.

To sailing folk, coming up the Orwell from Harwich, it is their gateway into Suffolk. To the shorebound holidaymaker it is an introduction to a land that is different from any other county—different in colour and scenery; and even the light in the skies is something which many an artist, including Constable, has striven to reproduce on canvas. There are no horses like Suffolk horses, a breed being saved by a society of enthusiasts. Their terrific pulling powers are known all over the world. Stan Rogers, said by some to be one of the finest horsemen in Suffolk, lived by the Pin Mill shore and once told me:—"You can lead 'em anywhere, but you can't drive 'em and it's the same with us."

A Suffolk Punch, as the breed is called, has been known to go almost down on his knees to shift a load such as no other horse could tackle. He will not give up. And if you upset the horseman you'll get a Suffolk punch on the nose.

No writer can tell you everything about Suffolk. There is too much to tell. But I hope this book has given the reader a slice to taste.

Author at the wheel of the *Cambria*.

Index